When we know who we are in Christ, we become a light in a hurting world searching for self-worth. In Be You Beloved, Miranda leads you by the hand on the expedition of revealing the lies of the enemy that keep each of us from being everything that we were created to be. Through personal stories, Biblical truth, and life application, Miranda trailblazes the adventure to discover our destiny as God's treasured ones. If you have ever questioned who you are, or your value, you can be sure to find insight and answers here!

- **Natasha Tubbs**, MDiv., MA., BCCC, speaker and author of *In Pursuit of Purpose*

I0167898

## What people are saying about
### *Be You, Beloved*

When Jesus walked the earth, he brought real solutions that released hope, liberating people free from the heaviest chains of oppression and shame through the power of love. He came full of grace and truth, leading the broken and confused to discover who they were from an encounter with Himself, God in the flesh. The Lord hasn't changed and is raising up voices on the earth to declare what God is like and how valuable we are to Him. I believe Miranda Trudeau is one of those voices. In Be you, Beloved you will find practical keys to flush lies, make an agreement with truth, and begin to walk in a truer version of yourself full of hope, self-love and an authentic expression of who you really are.

- **Tom Crandall**, author of *Your Life Speaks*, youth director of Young Saints at Bethel Church, Redding CA

There is a growing crisis of identity today. Young and old, male and female alike, this confusion, discouragement, feeling of lack, depression, and inadequacy picks any age and gender to torment and subdue. But God is revealing answers in this hour to those who are seeking solutions. This book is just that, a well laid-out, honest, and vulnerable writing of Miranda's journey in overcoming the lies of the enemy, often placed in her mind at a young age through well-meaning friends, cruel classmates, and even random strangers. In my opinion, everyone should read this book, but it will be exceptionally helpful and powerful to teens wrestling with their identity. Thank you Miranda for this book and your honesty!

- **Jay and Krista Armaly**, senior pastors at Antioch Christian Ministries

Knowing your identity is central to living a life of victory in Christ. It's vital that we know who God is and who we are in Christ if we want to lead a life that impacts the world around us. In Miranda's book, *Be You, Beloved* she shares truth, personal examples, and opportunities for you to process and discover who you are. Most of us have had harmful words spoken over us in the past, and this book can bring you into a place of freedom and truth in who God says you are.

- **Anna Maher**, author of *Embracing Mystery*

Miranda is a new voice that shares out of conviction, passion, and her story. There's an honesty available when we look to bring people into the freedom that we've found, and *Be You, Beloved* does exactly that. It's an invitation into an upgrade of freedom, identity and confidence in who you are. This book includes encouragement and clarity for the next steps in discovering not just who you are but whose you are. We are proud to recommend this book for anyone who wants to discover more of who they are in Christ!

- **Drew and Melissa Neal**, senior leaders at Generation ONE

# Be You, Beloved

## Overcoming lies & uncovering your true identity

**Miranda Trudeau**

*Be You, Beloved* —Copyright ©2019 by Miranda Trudeau
Published by Tru House Press

All rights reserved. No portion of this book may be reproduced or shared in any form—electronic, printed, photocopied, recording, or by any information storage and retrieval system, without prior written permission from the publisher. The use of short quotations is permitted.

Scripture quotations are from the ESV® Bible (The Holy Bible, English Standard Version®), copyright © 2001 by Crossway, a publishing ministry of Good News Publishers. Used by permission. All rights reserved.

ISBN 979-8-218-84205-5

Interior Design:
Matt Russell, Marketing Image, mrussell@marketing-image.com

Printed in the United States of America
2019—First Edition
2025—Second Edition

*To my husband, Jeffrey,*

*Thank you for putting up with the late nights writing and editing, and all of the times I refused to call you "Jeff" and instead settled on "Jefe", "Jeffrey", and "Lucas".*

*You truly are my biggest supporter, and without you, this book wouldn't have happened.*

*Now, go ahead and enjoy one uninterrupted bag of Jalapeno Cheetos – and I won't even make a face and tell you how terrible they smell. You're welcome.*

*Love you, Lucas.*

# CONTENTS

# FOREWORD

We're not meant to do this life alone, and every once in a while, our paths intersect with a person who leaves a lasting impression. A few years ago, I was running a ministry at my local church, and one morning, I had a large event to set up for. I arrived early and quickly started checking things off my long to-do list. As I frantically worked, an unfamiliar young lady approached me, unprompted, and energetically asked, "Hey, what can I do to help you?" My first impression of Miranda Trudeau was undoubtedly *this girl is awesome, and she gets things done*—without being asked—I might add. Miranda sees a need and addresses it.

Fast forward a few years and Miranda not only writes books but also works on a publishing team, coaching other authors throughout the writing and publishing process. Authoring a book is not for the faint of heart. Among writers, and people everywhere, there is a great need to be mentored, prayed for, and constantly encouraged. Miranda saw this need and decided to once again step up to the plate, partnering with and mentoring writers to fully walk in the truth of who they are in Christ. The result of someone walking in their Kingdom identity is a life-giving person, shining bright in the world, bringing healing, love, and wholeness everywhere they go.

In *Be You, Beloved*, Miranda shares about knowing and embracing your God-given identity, your Kingdom identity, so that you become the best version of yourself. Miranda is uniquely qualified in so many ways to share this message because she lives it. She saw a need in her own life for healing and wholeness, so she pressed in and found out what God truly thinks of her according to His Word. She's never been the same. She sees needs in every community she is a part of, and she works to meet those needs. With this book, she's on a mission to make sure everyone knows how crazy in love God is with humanity and the things that can be accomplished because of His love.

I encourage you to open your heart to what God wants to do in you, your relationships, and your community through the truths shared in this book. Discover who you are and let the love, health, and the power God has for you personally to fill and infiltrate every part of your being. As you begin to discover who you truly are, you'll discover gifts you never knew you had. And guess what? Those gifts you possess are supposed to be used to meet needs. Remember how I mentioned Miranda sees a need then she meets it? She's about to teach you to do the same. The world is FULL of needs, and in order to meet them, you must embrace a healthy identity and "Be You."

- **Amber Olafsson**, author of *THE AWESOME ONE*, owner of UNITED HOUSE Publishing

## LETTER TO THE READER

Dear Friend,

I challenge you to look at your life. Take a moment and think of all the relationships you have. Think of all the people you interact with on a daily basis. You have parents, friends, family, co-workers, teachers, and more. Think of what you've walked through with these people, which relationships are struggling now, which ones you don't understand, and in which ones, you're searching for more. That's why I'm here.

At the foundation of everything, I believe there is more. I believe that Christ intended greatness and wholeness for you, redemption and restoration. I believe these intentions go further than the actions of the cross; they apply to your life here in this time as well. You aren't called to simply wait around for Him to come get you; you are called to pursue the Kingdom and bring Heavenly perspectives to earth. I'm not sure why you're here, but I can guess there is a small urge inside of you that says, "There is more to life than this," and you want to figure out where it is coming from.

This process of discovering "the more" includes developing a healthy view of your identity, a healthy view of who God made others to be, and a healthy view of what your responsibilities are in your relationships. If you have relationships that don't seem to be going the way you'd like, this is for you, and I am here to help.

I have lived my whole life searching for a way to have positive and healthy relationships. I have found myself in situation after situation, relationship after relationship, stuck in this cycle of unhealthiness that I couldn't figure out how I got into or how to get out of. I continually found myself in places where I was treated poorly, and most of the time (if I am honest with myself), I walked right into them expecting it to be different.

"This one will work out," I told myself.
"This person won't hurt me," I told myself.
"This time it will be different," I told myself.

Sound familiar?

I repeated these statements knowing deep in my heart that nothing was going to change. I trusted people too much who didn't deserve to be given pieces of my heart, yet I gave these parts of me away freely, just hoping someone would help me find healing and restoration. This manifested itself through me being dependent, needy, and too emotional in relationships in order to garner attention and satisfaction from another person, all in an effort to fill me up in some way.

But God's plan is different. His intention for all is restoration, wholeness, and healthiness. This is exactly what Christ embodied when He came to the earth—how to have healthy relationships even in the midst of an unhealthy and broken world. If you take a close look at it, Jesus stepped into this world and completely engaged the culture. He partnered with the disciples and his followers and looked around to figure out what people needed.

He evaluated what they were experiencing, where they were struggling, and what they needed help redefining. He saw where they fell short in their weakness and where they were strong. His end goal was restoration. He wanted to show His people what it meant to be healthy and whole; He wanted to restore them to Himself and His Father so the love and purity God intended for the world could be maintained. He came to fulfill the law and create a new way for us, a better way.

So, how do we stop the unhealthy cycles? How do we bring Heavenly perspective for relationships here to earth? How do we step out of where we currently are and into "the more" that God has for us? How do we even begin to believe there is more available for us in our lives?

No "one-time fix" is guaranteed, you have to put your heart into it. You can read this book cover to cover a thousand times, but that won't change the fact that in order to create real change, Christ is calling you to commit and yield to the process. He is calling you forward into a better way, and this takes both understanding and action. It takes partnering with Him in all you are doing, even beyond relationships. If you want more in your life, you have to trust Him above all else—because without Him, none of this would be possible.

I am excited for the journey this book will take you on. I am excited for the thought processes this will spark, for the new ideas you will begin to form, and ultimately, for the deepened relationship you will have with your Father at the end of it all. I don't claim to have all the answers, and I don't claim to know perfectly how to walk this all out, but I am offering you my perspective, my stories, and my tools to help you navigate successfully through life and relationships.

This book will touch heavily on your identity, because if I have learned anything, it is that identity is everything. Healthy relationships aren't possible if you don't have a healthy view of who you are in Christ. If you come away with nothing else from this book, I want you to understand who you *really* are. Your identity gives way to the people you attract, the relationships you sustain, and the actions you take when situations are unhealthy. If your view of yourself is limited or broken, you will never reach the full quality of relationships as intended by Christ.

Beyond that, I will walk through some unique points in the creation story, some exercises you can do to be more intentional in your relationships, and tell all-too-revealing stories about my life in order to help you walk through yours. I will encourage you, lift you up, and spur you on toward all that Christ has for you.

My dream is for this book to help you re-learn how to be you by re-discovering who He says you are. Always remember, there is more because of Him.

With encouragement,
Mir

# WHO
*you are*

"We have the ability, responsibility, and the right to choose who speaks identity to us. No one steals that seat, we invite them."

# 1

# **What**
*they said*

As children, our view of who we are is shaped by what those around us say. Those influential adults who've spoken about life, those mean kids at school whose words stung, that cute girl or boy in class whose every word we clung to. All of these different people spoke into who we believed we were as children, and we often carry these messages about our identity into our adulthood. Parents especially have an important role in this. Whether you had a healthy relationship with your parents and they spoke positively into your life or a negative relationship that was filled with shame, condemnation, and insults, every word they said rests deep in your heart and sits at your core.

I remember I was on the bus once, and these kids started making fun of my glasses. As a child, these moments seem like the end of the world, right? I got glasses in fourth grade, and while getting braces seemed cool, getting glasses seemed dorky. I was labeled from an early age by something so simple and medically necessary, but it changed my perspective of myself for a long time. I was convinced through most of my schooling years that I could never be cool because I had glasses. It wasn't until I was about ready to graduate high school that I was able to get contacts, so for many years, I personally experienced the effect that others' words can have on you.

As we get older, the list of who takes a spot in the judgment seat expands. Teachers, professors, bosses, current friends, ex-friends, ex-boyfriends or girlfriends, the barista at the coffee shop, neighbors, grandmas, grandpas, pastors, the list goes on and on. Even now, there are voices constantly flowing at us on a daily basis, and if we don't learn to manage the volume we allow those voices to have, we will be left with our heads spinning and our hearts hurting.

I believe part of the reason that we can have such trouble digging out what is at our core and allowing ourselves to discover our true identity is our unique journeys from childhood to adulthood. When you enter this world as a child, you are completely and utterly dependent on your caregivers. You need them for food, water, clothing, housing, all of it. As you grow older, you become more independent, and in this part of the process, parents let go little by little as they teach you how to survive on your own. Even though this process looks a bit different for everyone, we all end up in adulthood. Then you are responsible for your own bills, your own food, and your own sustenance.

Through middle school and high school, I had a really hard time letting go of dependence on others. That innate childhood pattern didn't die easily with me, because to be honest, I don't think I trusted myself fully. I thought if I stopped looking at others and really looked at myself, I wouldn't like what I saw. I didn't believe

I could get through these years without copying my friends or without continually depending on others for my validation. In so many other instances, I was the most responsible person my age. I had a lot of younger siblings, and as the oldest, it came with a natural amount of responsibility that I had to accept. Despite this, I didn't feel qualified to handle life. I didn't feel empowered to make decisions, to stand up for what I deeply believed in, or to take control and live my life out of who I knew God made me to be. It was a heart issue that caused my actions to reflect what I really thought about myself, instead of the truth of who I was.

What about you?

**What are a few positive things you remember people saying about you? Who said them?**

_____

_____

_____

_____

_____

_____

**What are a few negative things you remember people saying about you? Who said them?**

_____

_____

_____

_____

_____

**Who would you say were the top three voices that spoke into your life as a child?**

1. _____

2. _____

3. _____

Does any of this resonate? I am asking these questions and saying all of this because I want you to understand how it can play a role in the whole process of walking out of healthiness in your life. Figuring out who we believe we are is crucial to evaluating our relationships and learning what healthiness looks like in action – and this starts with looking back at our childhood. This type of reflection will help us understand not only what formed our opinions of ourselves from the beginning, but also how we acted in situations as a young person. Ultimately, our expressions of ourselves reflect what we think about ourselves.

**Our expressions of ourselves reflect what we think about ourselves.**

Let me be clear, just because we think something about ourselves does not mean it's truth. Feelings and truth are two separate things, and we have to realize this as we proceed forward. Feeling like you are incapable of something doesn't absolve the truth that you are created for greatness, that you are created to be powerful, and that you are capable of achieving. Rather than setting up camp in what we think about ourselves, we can find strength to walk through the lies and step into our true identities in Christ, as we learn to recognize when our feelings are saying something different than what He says about us.

As we walked through childhood, there were so many voices around us. These don't decrease as we get older, and I am sure you could come up with at least ten voices who speak into your life on a consistent basis. What would it look like if we lived with authority and power to turn down those voices? Think about this for a second—we have the ability, the responsibility, and the right to choose who speaks identity to us. No one steals that seat; WE get to invite them in because ultimately, we can decide where we find our identity. It is so necessary that we take control over this portion of our lives.

I don't know your story or what type of voices you had speaking into your life. I had a mix—some people spoke positive things, but there were many other voices that I allowed to speak freely in their negativity. From the teacher who declared I would never be able to take a test successfully, to the leader who said I would never be good enough to help. These negative words, along with many others, planted seeds in my heart and developed roots that spread so deep that many of them still rest there. I was hurting; I was broken, and it took me a long time to heal from the labels that had been tattooed on my heart. For so long, my past experiences were a huge roadblock in ever discovering the "more" that God had planned for me, and it definitely delayed me from really coming into partnership with who He says I am. I sat in brokenness, not really expecting that change would come, but hoping and believing in my heart that it would happen all at once, unexpectedly, without any work on my part. I quickly learned otherwise, realizing that my actions were as much needed as my open heart, and I came to learn that with work and effort, I could uncover the lies of the enemy about my identity and really step into my God-given identity. It was a journey that I am so glad I took and one I hope to take you on throughout this book.

## BREAKING UP WITH THE LIES

How many of these lies of the enemy are you believing?

You aren't worthy.
You aren't good enough.
You're ugly.
You never do a good job.
You always mess up.
You're a failure.

**What influences in your life led you to believe these lies?**

_____

_____

_____

I'm sure the list could go on so much longer, but whether spoken directly or indirectly to you, these phrases can cut deep and live long in the places they develop roots. They can resurface when that date doesn't call you back, or that boss doesn't hire you, or that relationship you thought was the "real thing" doesn't pan out the way you believed and hoped and dreamed it would. These phrases come back, and one moment of rejection can lead to your mind spinning with these declarations about who other people say you are.

Then, something happens, and you start to mentally say "yes" to the narrative that someone else was writing about you. A new moment of rejection partners with the old declarations about who you are, and you're left thinking:

"Wow, I guess I'm not worthy; they were right."
"Wow, I guess I'm not good enough; they were right."
"Wow, I guess I am ugly; they were right."
"Wow, I guess I never do a good job; they were right."
"Wow, I guess I do always mess up; they were right."
"Wow, I guess I am a failure; they were right."

What an unfortunate, messy, and all-too-real shift. You may begin to judge yourself and come into agreement with what other people have said as truth. Then, what they once said about you, or demonstrated to you in how they've acted in your relationships, might become what you wholeheartedly believe about yourself. Their declaration becomes your belief. Now, you repeat over and over to yourself in your heart:

I'm not worthy.
I'm not good enough.
I'm ugly.
I never do a good job.
I always mess up.
I'm a failure.

THIS. IS. NOT. YOUR. IDENTITY.

Those statements are not your identity. Those declarations are not who you truly are. I have seen far too many people stop short of realizing these statements are false. So many have pitched a tent in this broken view and stopped trying to reach for a truthful belief about who they are. This seems logical given that every single attempt to figure out truth has been crushed. Their hope has been stolen, and their positivity is gone. They are left believing at their core these statements about themselves. They wholeheartedly embrace that this brokenness is their identity.

If you can relate, this is NOT where God intends for you to stay. Know that this brokenness is a circumstance, not an identity.

**Brokenness is a circumstance, not an identity.**

Those statements above? Those are NOT who He created you

to be. There is more, and there will always be more in Him. There is hope, and there will always be hope in Him. I hope to provide you with truths and encouragement about who you really are, walking this out with you, even when you don't really believe or understand it all right now. I hope to remind you of your truest identity, the one that the Creator of all has instilled in you from the very beginning; the Maker who knit you together in your mother's womb from the very first day. You can change your perspective. That heavy fog can lift, and you can welcome truth into your life.

You. Can. Do. This.

Start by writing out some positive thoughts towards yourself. Take this step of acknowledging that there is more to you than you currently understand—there is more to you than you've believed in the past. These thoughts could include positive things people have spoken over you, a favorite thing about yourself, or something you do well/are gifted in. Then, pray. Pray that God continues to expand this list in your heart. Pray that God would continue to reveal His thoughts about you daily.

**What is one thing God spoke to you while reading this chapter, and what steps are you going to take to engage Him more in this area?**

_____

_____

_____

_____

_____

_____

_____

_____

_____

_____

_____

# 2

# **What**
*you say*

I absolutely love my Google Home. My husband and I bought it about a year ago, and such a simple thing has become a joy to have. I'm not promoting here, but I love that I can ask a question or give direction, and in an instant, my Google device can make it happen. "Hey Google, play this hit song." "Hey Google, what's the weather?" "Hey Google, give me a hug," just kidding—it has its limits—but I think this example has a God-parallel.

Have you ever noticed that when something is "declared," it takes on a whole new form of power? It is almost as if what is being said is then spoken into being, whether positive or negative. I think back to the creation story in Genesis where God's power was showcased through life-creating words. Like the Google Home, I can only imagine that this is how God felt when He walked out creation—He spoke, and things happened! Think about it; everything that was created started as nothing. All He did was speak and mountains were formed, fish were flipping, birds were flying, and leaves were falling (fall is my favorite season, so I'm going to go ahead and believe it was fall 100% of the time in Eden). His words held a power unlike any other—the power to create. Given that we are made in the image and likeness of God, this is a strength we also carry, and that is why I believe declarations are so powerful.

Our words are powerful, and just as fun and positive creations can come from them, the negative power is real as well. One phrase I struggle with saying the most is, "I literally just can't." As funny and humorous as it is, I have found it to be a bit dangerous, and my husband recognized it too. Declarations are so authoritative, and even those made in jokes can plant negative seeds and lead your heart to start believing them. I'm now at the point where EVERY TIME my husband hears me say these things, he immediately stops me and makes me take it back and replace it with something positive. It seems silly, but it is so important, and I am so grateful to have someone in my life to help me recognize the power of positivity. Remember: your words create, so speak life over yourself, your body image, your relationships, your situations, everything.

If we recognize that our words are powerful, we must recognize that other people's words are powerful as well. When others speak negative things over us, our first outward reaction may be disgust or disagreement, but even the little words leave us with a very tiny seed planted in our hearts. This seed may begin to form roots, deepening its influence over us and resurfacing at the worst of times. When this happens, we begin to partner with those words from others, creating even deeper negative roots that can really damage how we see ourselves, and in turn, how we act in relationships. This all seems unstoppable, this negative cycle of identity, but don't lose hope because the truth is this:

if we let what other people say control what we think about ourselves, we are giving up power.

**If we let what other people say control what we think about ourselves, we are giving up power.**

We cannot control *what* other people say, I know this. We can always, always, always, however, control what we do with what they say. Negativity has a larger impact than we think, so it is important to recognize this now. No matter how many encouraging voices we may have speaking into us, we all have to learn how to turn the volume down on the negative ones. We could have the most supportive system around us speaking healthily into our lives, but just one adverse statement can take all that positivity and leave us drifting out in the sea without an anchor of truth. The destructive statements supersede the life-giving when we don't take the control needed to change the story. We have the power to change the story.

So, how do we stop the cycle?
How exactly do we change the story?
How do we take control of the narrative that has been spoken over our lives?

One thing I have found helpful is to write out five to ten daily declarations. These can alternate day by day, or they can be the same ones you repeat every time. When I used to do yoga, this is something I loved about the practice. Most of the practices are based around a mantra, and I would carry over my spiritual truths. I would choose a declaration that aligned with truth, and I would repeat it over, and over, and over again. I found affirmations in the Word that reinforced who He says I am, who He created me to be, and what He has called me to. I found positivity in those pages that helped me surface those lies which were spoken over me and gave me the confidence and power to take control of the narrative in a way I never had before. The central key to this part of the journey is to let go of what others have said and hang on tight to what He says.

**When you think of yourself, specifically who you believe you are, what three things come to mind first?**

1.
_____

2.
_____

3.
_____

Beyond what we say about ourselves, how do we stop partnering with what other people say about us?

To un-link from their conclusions, we have to re-link with something else, something positive. For so long, I partnered with what people were saying, which always let me down in the end. Even an encouraging relationship or a really healthy person can experience negative days, and because of this, I have learned that partnering with what people say about us is never a good idea. My husband is a great guy, but if I am constantly relying on him for my self-worth and feelings of success, his bad days will be my bad days too. We have to find something constant, trustworthy, solid, and unchanging to partner with in order to develop a healthy identity of who we are. We have to find something powerful enough to always speak rock-solid truth, help us heal from the lies, and help us dig up those roots that are planted so deep. We have to find something that instills our true identity in us and reminds us of who we *really* are daily.

The only consistent, reliable, and truth-filled voice that we can depend on is God's. He created us, He intended us for greatness, and He, over all, knows who we were made to be. In the next chapter, I will explore what He says about us. I will go all the way back to the origin of our true identity and explore what it is He thinks about us on a daily basis, even when we mess up.

**What is one thing God spoke to you while reading this chapter, and what steps are you going to take to engage Him more in this area?**

_____

_____

_____

_____

_____

_____

# 3

# **What**
*God says*

Recently, Jeffrey and I went to his 10-year high school reunion, and you know what I noticed? How often the phrase, "How are you?" was used. Now, I completely believe that these people were trying to be nice and see how we were doing, but I don't really think they wanted or would have been prepared had we given a completely truthful answer. Have you ever experienced that? Growing up in church, this used to happen all of the time. I would get so frustrated when I was going through something tough, feeling like I couldn't really say anything other than, "I'm fine" in response to this question. Can you relate? This is simply one example, but so often, we say phrases because it seems appropriate—and not because we have taken the time to truly examine the reality behind the phrase.

I see the same thing happen with the phrase, "Jesus loves you." Don't get me wrong, it is an extremely crucial and central part to the Gospel, but if you're anything like me, after you hear it so many times, you start to become numb to it. The more you hear it, the more it simply becomes something you say in your life, in your church, or to someone who is hurting. After a while, these words lose value to us, and we miss the meaning, the truth, and the sacrifice behind this profound statement. In turn, when things aren't going as planned, or when something devastating happens, we begin to doubt if this is really truth. Anxiety replaces this reality with doubt, and we end up saying, "Me? That's impossible," "I've done the WORST thing ever," or, "I have broken all ten of the Ten Commandments. There is no way that statement applies to me." Well, it does. It took a long time for me to re-realize the glorious fact that He really does love me (and you). He loved you from the moment He thought you up, followed by when He took time to knit you together, all the way to when you made your grand entrance into the earth, and every day after. He has just been waiting for you to realize how AMAZING and valued you are, so you can partner with Him and accomplish all you were purposed for. He thought of you, created you, and then sat back and watched as His glorious child entered this earth with a deep breath and a cry, ready to take on all that was laid before you. Yes, you have sinned. Yes, you've had struggles, but none of that can top the fact that you are HIS child, and His goal is to remind you of that each day, so you can live even more for Him as every moment passes.

This is how I like to think about it. Right after a baby is born, it takes a large breath, exhales, and lets out a loud cry, alerting its parents that it's here, it's healthy, and its lungs work. That magical moment of life is fueled by none other than our Heavenly Papa. I love to imagine what joy He feels when we begin life here, at that moment when His Heavenly creation touches earth and the two merge into one. That first breath of life the baby takes, the breath straight from its Creator, fuels its existence into every moment after. This is the breath that will power its words, the breath that will create its first laugh, the breath that will fuel it to say "mama" and "dada." This powerful breath from the best Daddy we could ever have flows through each baby's lungs, giving it life.

This isn't some phenomenon that ends with infancy. Our Father, though in Heaven, is near to us, and He is the one who provides that first breath of life and every single breath after. As you walk through school, relationships, jobs, and family of your own, that breath is the one that rests deep inside of you, reminding you of the power and love you have access to all the days of your life. This breath doesn't only come when we are newborns searching for oxygen. It is always accessible, there to sustain our existence as we walk out life on this earth. If we realize and tap into this daily, we are bound to have powerful and purpose-filled outcomes because when we partner with the Father, He will give us the desires of our hearts.

## YOU ARE REDEEMED

One of my favorite things to reflect on is when Adam spent time with God in the Garden of Eden before all of the nakedness, disappointments, evil, and destruction. Kind of like that calm before the storm type of feeling—like the moment where you have your coffee on the couch, early in the morning, the phones are all silenced, nobody is awake in the house yet, and you are just, resting. Recouping. Relaxing. Restoring. That is what I picture it being like with Adam. He got to spend time with God, exploring the Garden, naming animals, getting to know Eve, enjoying his fresh cup of coffee (I fully believe coffee is a Heavenly product).

Then the "storm" hits. The serpent comes, and hell breaks loose.

Adam and Eve lost sight of who God was and tried to compensate on their own, and what was their first reaction? Shame.

Ugh. What an ugly, ugly word. Shame. It creeps up at the worst times and is caused by some negative situation we feel we have created or played a role in. Adam and Eve made a mistake, and sin entered the world. In my reflection, this would have been a *great* moment for God to say, "Oh, well this is NOT what I expected. I wasn't prepared for this; I didn't want this. NO. NO. NO. These people aren't worth it." But is that what He did? Not even in the slightest. There were consequences, as there are to all actions, BUT GOD never left us. He didn't walk away. He didn't call us unworthy. He knew our TRUE identity, and how we were intended to live.

God did everything He could to maintain a relationship with us. There are books and books in the Bible detailing covenants He made with His people, designed to bring us closer to Him, to give us a greater glimpse of His character, and ultimately, to restore us. I believe with all my heart that God could have snapped His fingers, made Satan disappear, and restored all back to what was intended originally through Eden. I believe with all my heart that He is all-powerful—of course He is, He is God. However, I know that His plan was bigger, that He works all together for good, and I am in awe that God saw this as the perfect opportunity to show us His love. He gave us the *beauty* of choice, and what a beauty that is.

With choice, there is inherent freedom. God's desire is not to restrict us, control us, or isolate us from everything in this world—He *created* this world. In John 3:16 it says, "For God so loved the world, that he gave his only Son..."; He loved the whole world—not just the people who loved Him back at that moment. He wants to let us be free, to watch us grow and laugh and learn and chase after Him, to make our own decision to run toward Him with all our strength and to make this relationship our number one priority. He wants to watch as we live our lives demonstrating the values of Heaven and the characteristics of His nature. His desire isn't to create separation between us and the world, but to give us options that result in us making powerful choices, choices that can bring God's Kingdom to earth.

Back to Genesis for a minute. In the wake of all that destruction, God saw the opportunity to show us something. Despite His almighty power and ability to reverse it all back, He chose a different way. He chose to send His Son. Christ dying for us was an act of love and restoration to show us just how much we mean to Him, to show us His power, His love, His mercy, His grace, and most of all, how much we are worth to Him. Remember that shame? He died and rose again to show us that sin and shame isn't who we are, that isn't what we should feel, and that isn't AT ALL what our identity is based in. If He could look at the situation Adam and Eve had created and redeem it, can't He redeem yours, too?

Our true identity is rooted in how He sees us, and we have to train ourselves to only see what He sees. As I said before, we CANNOT base our identity or foundation on what other people are saying about us or how other people treat us. The only true source of identity is Christ, and through the act on the cross, He provided us with access to an undeniable and beautiful power through Him. His heart is redemption and restoration, so cling to that and let Him tell you who He made you to be.

These things may not all seem positive right now, but it's

important to be honest with yourself about where you are. In the next sections, I am going to walk through real, tangible truths of what God says about you. An essential part of this process is to be truthful with yourself about the current state you are in, but it's equally and possibly even more important to be willing to listen to what God thinks about you as well.

Start by writing out three declarations that align with the truth of who God says you are. I encourage you to take this list and expand it!

Here are some scriptures to check out that will help you—it's always important to go to the Father and ask Him, and the words He declares over us in the Bible are a great place to start!

Psalm 139:14
Jeremiah 31:3
Isaiah 43:1
John 8:36
Ephesians 5:1

## YOU ARE WORTHY

**Write out three declarations that align with the truth of who God says you are.**

**I am**
_____

**I am**
_____

**I am**
_____

Christ instilled worth in us the moment He gave His life for us. Think about it. If we weren't worth ANYTHING, would He have done what He did? Christ's sacrifice instilled dignity in us. We may not have deserved it, but He saw us worthy enough anyway. God gave up His ONLY Son. He gave up one third of the trinity for... death? No. For you and me.

Because He believes in who you are.
He believes in what you can do.
He believes in who He made you to be.

That large of an act ascribed worth to us, so we are worthy.

You. Are. Worthy.

Believing this is step one to building a great foundation of your true identity. The most frequent lie I've encountered in our society is the one that tells me I am not enough. As a woman, I can look around every corner and see a new example of what is "hot," what is "not," and a full ten-page article telling me which category I should be in. We are in a constant state of comparison that leads so many of us to the conclusion that we are not worth anything. So many young people walk through years not thinking they have any worth, and almost all of us have walked through a season of struggling to figure out what makes us feel worthy.

What instills worth for you? What makes you feel worthy and valuable? Is it new clothes? The shiniest car? The biggest engagement ring? Compliments? Likes on social media? What is it? Think about it for a second. What causes that "pleasure" receptor to go off in your brain and give you a taste of this thing called "worth?" In what moments do you feel most qualified and like you have the most authority? This could range from something as consistent as your job to as rare as winning an award.

I am not saying that these things are bad by any means. The Lord delights in our success, and He is the One who created us with drive and creativity. Delighting in your accomplishments isn't negative, but when those accomplishments begin to define your identity, you may find yourself in dangerous territory. When we don't feel inherently worthy, we work to get our worth. Thankfully, the Kingdom of God isn't one based on works because He did it all. Jesus said, "It is finished," and He meant it. We don't have to strive to prove that we are worthy, and if we are stuck in this cycle, we need to revisit our foundational truths about where our identity comes from. We have to ask ourselves, "Do I really believe that God calls me worthy? Do I really believe that His approval is not something I have to work to gain?"

I can guarantee you that He does call you worthy and that you do not have to work to find His approval, but I encourage you to talk to your Papa about what He thinks of you. Explore what He has said about His people through Scriptures, and ultimately, ask Him, "Papa, what do you think about me? Am I worthy?"

Here are a few verses, but I encourage you to search His Word to find even more:

"For I know the plans I have for you, declares the Lord, plans for welfare and not for evil, to give you a future and a hope." Jeremiah 29:11 ESV

"Your eyes saw my unformed substance; in your book were written, every one of them, the days that were formed for me, when as yet there were none of them. How precious to me are your thoughts, O God! How vast is the sum of them! If I would count them, they are more than the sand. I awake, and I am still with you." Psalm 139:16-17 ESV

"Are not two sparrows sold for a penny? And not one of them will fall to the ground apart from your Father. But even the hairs on your head are all numbered. Fear not, therefore; you are of more value than many sparrows." Matthew 10:29-31 ESV

Learn to commune in the peace and love that He has for you and watch as your heart is changed.

## YOU ARE POWERFUL

This is one value I struggled with for a long time. I know one of the biggest problems I had in my past relationships was that I gave away the power. I let other people have the opportunity to tell me who I was, what I should do, and how I should act. Growing up, I was always considered a follower not a leader. I wasn't the one at the head of the popular group at school; I was the one following closely behind trying to mimic their every move to figure out what I needed to look like to fit in. I handed my power to the girl who looked the prettiest, the guy who talked the sweetest, the friend who seemed to have the most influence, etc. There wasn't a moment in those situations where I had enough self-worth or a high enough self-esteem to take the power for myself and be confident enough to uniquely live out my own life.

It took me a long time to realize that God created me to be powerful, and in the meantime, I spent a lot of my life clinging to the strength and success of other people. The truth is, He made us to have power and authority. On a basic level, we are His representatives here, with the intention of bringing the Kingdom to earth. We aren't here to sit around and wait for Jesus to return and take us to Heaven, but instead we are called to action. Right before Jesus left this earth, He imparted to his disciples the famous Great Commission, calling them to "Go therefore and make disciples of all nations," (Matthew 28:19 ESV). He wanted them to GO. Even after He was taken up, the disciples were just standing around (not going), so God sent an angel that was like, "Hey, whatcha doin? Jesus said go... so... so..." (my translation). Even the command of making disciples of nations is one that calls for great power. How were the disciples supposed to fulfill a calling like that if they weren't given some capacity and authority to bring Jesus' Kingdom and Heavenly values to earth?

This same calling applies to us, which means that we are called to have the same power and authority in order to spread the true values of Jesus wherever we go.

"For God gave us a spirit not of fear but of power and love..." 2 Timothy 1:7a ESV

"But you will receive power when the Holy Spirit has come upon you..." Acts 1:8a ESV

"Truly, truly, I say to you, whoever believes in me will also do the works that I do; and greater works than these..." John 14:12a ESV

This all reveals a beautiful fact about God. Despite what you may have heard or what you may have been taught, God doesn't want to take the power from us; He wants to empower us to live as He created us to live. As we talked about before, He knows our original intention (because He created us), and because of Christ, He doesn't see all of our sin when He looks at us; He sees us solely for how we were meant to be, for who we really are to Him in this Heavenly perspective. HOW EMPOWERING!

Let me clarify what power is. I am not intending for you to perceive that powerful people are mean people. People who are mean in relationships, though they may appear strong, are actually fearful underneath. Fear directs people to have the need to control, condemn, and destroy. Jesus was the perfect example of a man who had real power. He walked with authority, carrying out His mission on this earth—to love and to guide people to Himself and the Father. To show people what Heaven's values truly were.

True power is to be humble, kind, graceful, honest, and loving. Power means to be confident enough in who you are that you don't need to control others. When you are truly a healthy person who has authority, you don't let insecurity control you, and you don't feel the need to control other people out of that insecurity. When you are walking in the empowerment of Heaven you are self-assured enough that you don't need to blindly follow people. You know who you were made to be, and you're living that out daily. You don't need someone else's validation to make decisions or to live your daily life because you simply know who your Papa created you to be and what He thinks of you—that He empowers you to be in control of your decisions, your actions, and your relationships.

## YOU ARE CONNECTED

I can't write a book about identity and not talk about connection. All relationships are based in identity. Who we are as relational people flows out of who we believe we are when no one is around. At our core, we all crave connection. From the time we are itty babies, straight from our mama, we want to feel linked to others. This desire is carried with us throughout our lives, manifesting itself in relationship after relationship. What if we were people that strongly bonded with every person we came in contact with? That would be crazy. Even as someone who LOVES people, I have to be in control of who I unite with, right? With our identity rooted in our worthiness and power, we can exercise our authority and live out our relationships as God intended.

God didn't create you to be controlled by other people; He created you to be in healthy relationships with other people. Have you ever heard the statement, "You are who you hang out with"? I don't fully believe this, but there is a nugget of truth to it. Not only do you adapt to those that are around you, but you also attract those who are like you. Healthy people want to be around healthy people, and unhealthy people group with other unhealthy people. This is why it is so crucial that we understand that identity comes first—always. Understanding who you are plays a role in all the connections that you have.

You may struggle with this now—I did for a long time—but I am believing that you can find your center with the Father and regroup. Centering your life around Christ starts with asking Him who you are. If you ask, He will tell. To give you a glimpse of what He has told me (and He thinks the same of you), here are some small beginnings:

You are loved.
You are dear to Him.
You are HIS child, and He would do anything for you.
You are beautiful.
You were NOT an accident.
You were created to be powerful and influential.
You have control.

I encourage you to take a notebook or piece of paper and write these out. As you do, reflect with your Papa on the truth in each of these statements. Take these as "I am" statements and revisit them weekly, or even daily. Read them, and repeat them over and over until they have rooted themselves deep in your heart and identity, there to carry you through everything that you do.

I am loved.
I am dear to You.
I am Your child and You would do anything for me.
I am beautiful.
I was NOT an accident.
I was created to have power and authority.
I have control.

There are so many more truths you can find not only in the Bible, but also in simple conversation with Him. He is your Heavenly Father, and He wants to talk to you.

**What is one thing God spoke to you while reading this chapter, and what steps are you going to take to engage Him more in this area?**

_____

_____

_____

_____

_____

_____

_____

_____

_____

_____

_____

# 4

# **What**
## *you believe*

Having a healthy view of yourself is crucial to starting this journey towards wholeness in your life. You need to understand who you really are, based on who your Father says you are. You have worth. You have power. You have authority. You have value.

The journey alone of learning to believe the truth about who you are is exactly that—a journey. It is a day-to-day process of waking up and choosing to love yourself. Marriage is one of the relationships where this choice needs to be most prevalent. Let me give you a little insight into what it looks like. Some single people I have come across view marriage as this amazing "feeling-fest." They can have a wrong perception and see it as two people who are so in love, so head-over-heels, so giddy with excitement, that they just *have* to be together for the rest of their lives. With that, they run to the altar in excitement and get married (after whatever length of time they've enjoyed dating). While some of that observation may be true, in reality, it's always half of the story. Marriage is about choosing your spouse. It is about waking up, day after day, looking next to you, and saying, "I am going to *choose* to love you, even when I don't feel like it. Even when you don't earn it. Even when I have every justified reason not to."

In the same way, you *must* choose to love yourself. It's not selfish or conceited or pretentious; it's healthy. You need to wake up every day, look yourself in the mirror, and say, "Today, I choose *you*. Today, I invest in *you*. Today, I will love *you*. No matter what happens, how you act, what you do, what mistakes you make, none of it. Regardless of all circumstances, I choose you." This is unconditional love. This is something we all need to learn, whether we have seen it exemplified in our relationships or not. We need this both for ourselves and for others.

One of the ways I choose myself is through alone time. To be honest, I am not the kind of person who likes to be alone. I love people, conversations, going out to eat with friends, having game nights, long phone calls—all of it. Despite my desperate love of being around people, however, I have learned that I *have* to take time for myself. I never thought I needed it, but I absolutely do. Every week, I make sure to take time alone, whether I am watching TV, playing a game on my phone, reading a book, writing a book, napping, whatever it is. I need some time alone, even from my husband, to simply be. In these moments, regardless of how insignificant they seem, I have learned who I am, what I like, and how to love myself. I have become more comfortable with myself at the core, without the influence of others all around, and those moments have become the powerful and solid foundation for everything else that I give my time to.

Take time for yourself, just try it. Take a shower, do some yoga, watch your favorite show, and relax. Just be you. Don't talk to anyone; don't answer your phone (in fact, I put it in a completely different room). Take an hour, a half hour, ten minutes to simply learn who you are. This is a crucial foundation for learning to love yourself, and when you take time to invest in you, it leaves you refreshed and refilled, so that you can invest in others.

## CHOOSE YOURSELF

The largest mental block I had to get over when I started this journey of intentionally investing in myself first is the lie that this choice is selfish—that choosing to care about myself is selfish. Think about this for a minute. Imagine that you lead an upper-level department at a large company and you are in charge of the yearly fundraiser. Your head has been spinning with tasks since the moment that you were given the job, and in the midst of it all, you first choose to focus on the guest list. This isn't necessarily a bad choice, but as time passes, you continue ONLY to focus on the people coming. In every party, you are networking. Every down minute you are talking with someone on the phone about who they are bringing and what they are wearing. Every focused moment is you writing down more contacts, and this is all good! You are going to have one of the most well-attended parties of the century because of your intentionality to build relationships, expand your network, and put yourself out there. You are investing time, and you are definitely seeing results.

Do you see where I'm going with this? What is the blind spot that you have in the planning of this party? There's no actual party! You may have the best guest list of any party in the world, but you didn't take the time to plan anything else for the evening. None of the foundational work was completed, and in turn, the party is going to fall apart, and all those relationships are now going to have a wedge in them. You built them on the expectation that there was an event taking place, and now there is no event. There is no DJ. There is no food. There are no keynote speakers. There are no raffles or packages to give away. In fact, other than the ticket prices, there is no other money coming in through this fundraiser!

This same situation can be transferred to your life. If you spend all your time investing in relationships and no time building your foundation, everything will fall apart. Taking care of yourself isn't selfish; it's necessary. You cannot sustain healthy relationships if you aren't first in a healthy state. You disperse to others the reality of what state your heart is in, so if you are running on an empty tank, it isn't possible for others to get the best version of you. Take time for yourself, as unimportant as it may seem. When you are dating, you invest time in getting to know the other person, and when you are married, you will take time to continually befriend your spouse, so expand on this example and do the same for you. Take time to sit with yourself. Learn what you like and dislike. Learn how to be patient and loving as you are in the process, and always remember that love covers all. I encourage you to post these on your fridge, tape them to your mirror, or frame them on your bedside table. You may need a reminder on a day-to-day basis to keep up with these, but it's important that you begin to make this a habit. You are worth it!

**When you think of yourself, of who you believe you are, what three things come to mind first?**

   **1.**
_____

**2.**

_____

**3.**

_____


## BE YOURSELF

Out of these foundation-building moments, you not only gain perspective on who you are, but you make better decisions overall. In these times, you are able to clear your mind and revisit your "why," and out of this, all your decisions will flow. You will give your "yes" to the best things in life, not just the good things. You will focus on what should be prioritized, and you won't feel pulled in a thousand directions every day. Most importantly, you are able to really put your best side into your relationships, giving the people around you not just a good version of yourself, but the best one.

When you neglect to take care of yourself, you will notice your relationships start to fall apart. As I said before, what you pour out to others is simply an overflow of the state of your heart.

**Whether they say it or not, people need you to be the best version of yourself.**

People need you to be prepared, confident, consistent, encouraging, and positive; these are just a few of the characteristics of a great friend. In reality, all of these features are developed out of the times where you build yourself (and allow God to rebuild what has been broken), where you start to create your solid foundation in those moments of establishing who you truly are. Each moment you spend time with God and allow him to pour into you, it fills you up a little more. It's like the gas tank of a car—every visit to the gas station, you're transferring fuel into your tank. Your tank could be half empty, ¾ empty, or if you're anything like me, it could be teetering on completely drained (I like to live life on the edge). Once your car is filled up, it then runs on the fuel you just purchased. The thing that powers each mile you drive is exactly what you just allowed into your tank, gasoline.

The same is true in Christ. When we are spending time consistently with God, He fills us with His life and His truth, and in turn, we become life-giving and truth-carrying people. Exactly what we allow to be poured into us, we will pour out. The more that we give God opportunities to fill our tank, the more confidence we will have in who we are and Whose we are. If we neglect these moments of connection, we are like a gas tank running on empty. So, in order to be the best version of yourself for the people around you, you need to be sure that what is powering each mile in your life is pure, full of truth, hope-filled, and life-giving.

## KNOW YOURSELF

Something that flows out of this alone time is the adventure of discovering your passion and your purpose. I believe that each of us are created by God with the ability to create. This is an aspect of God that was put inside each and every one of us when we were made in His image. I don't believe that we were all created with one singular purpose that we need to find specifically and carry out in our lives, but I do know that we are all capable of creating, cultivating, and exploring so many new, innovative, and unique things throughout our lifetime. We are all gifted in different ways, and only trial and error will reveal to you where your sweet spots lie, giving you a prime opportunity to pursue numerous dreams and goals that God has written personally on your heart.

Let me give you a little insight into my writing journey. I have dabbled in writing my whole life and have been blogging for a few years now, but nothing stuck. I was writing all of the time, but I wasn't feeling the ever-passionate desire to share it. Even when I did, I was never confident enough in the outcomes. Sound familiar? So many of us have dreams in our hearts that we let fear get ahold of. We have this far off desire that we think won't ever happen, but in reality, we are scared of what could occur if we did pursue it.

*What if we fail? What if it's not good enough? What if my family doesn't support it? What if nobody likes it? What if it is a waste of money? What if it is a waste of time? I should spend my time doing something productive, not writing a book, not making an album, not starting a business.*

The fear of the unknown is real, and especially when the unknown is a vulnerable state of our hearts' desire, we let this dream-killing fear grip us and stifle the dream altogether. Want some encouragement? There is no fear in Christ. " ... perfect love casts out fear" (1 John 4:18a ESV), leaving us with an environment where we can test and try things to our satisfaction, without fearing failure. We need to look at failure differently. It isn't messing up and discovering that you aren't good enough for something. I believe when we fail at something, it is an amazing opportunity to see where you tried, where you took a risk, and where now you can take everything you've learned from that experience and run with it into the next one. I approach failure as a moment of celebration, not one of sadness to be regretted.

This last year was my season of figuring out my "why." Your "why" is what motivates you. It's your passion. It's what helps you make decisions when you're faced with many good choices; it's the foundation behind what you are doing. My "why" is to help people cultivate healthiness in their life through encouragement and reaffirming their identity. This is why I write, why I letter, why I blog, why I put effort into these platforms—all to encourage you.

Once I had my why, the fears and discouragement about the outcomes disappeared—isn't that crazy? It is a feeling I never expected, but that entered my life all at once, changing absolutely everything. In the place of fear and discouragement, I found motivation and desire—to be consistent and encourage as many people as I could. I am by far not where I want to be yet, but I know where I'm headed because I know who I am, who He is, and what my why is.

The same goes for you, friend. I want to be honest with where I've been and where I am so that you know you're not alone in walking through this journey. The Creator of all intends more for us, and there is definitely more for you than you may believe there is. The possibilities in your life are great because He created you for greatness. The outcomes available for you are splendid because He created you for splendor. You are His beloved, and this relationship with your Papa can empower every aspect of your life, if you let it. He will speak passion over you; He will give you the desires of your heart as you delight in Him (Psalm 37:4), and as you live out of your God-given identity.

So what is your why? To get the wheels turning, I generally begin by asking people this question: "What breaks your heart?" Essentially, what motivates you? What sparks something inside of you that moves you to action? What burns so deep inside that you want to get out? The "what" is great, in fact, it is necessary. If you have a why without what, there is no action. If you live from the what, however, your life may have a lot of great outcomes, but you may be missing the why. What, overall, did you accomplish? What ultimate goal and purpose were you working for?

Remember that God doesn't do anything on accident, and in my experience, He always, always works everything together for good—no matter the circumstance. He uses it all. He may not have caused the hurtful relationship in your past, but you better believe that there is somebody in this world that needs to hear your story, someone that needs to see that you've gotten through it, and someone who will be encouraged that they can too. God uses it all. He uses your mistakes and your "failures." He uses your effort and your desires. He uses your heart and your passions. He uses your writing and your voice. He uses your business and your mind. He uses it all, the good and the bad, the pretty and the ugly.

Begin processing through what your why may be. There are so many good resources out there to help you walk through discovering it on a deeper level, but simply start by writing down what passions you have, what things you enjoy doing, what conversations you love having, what circumstances your heart breaks for, and what areas you have influence in. By looking at what specific experiences you have gone through and what special insights God has given you to use to help others, you can start to really figure out what your foundational why is.

Once you have your why then you can explore the what. So, sit down and brainstorm. Maybe your why is to bring light to a social issue—such as children and adults with special needs or assisting with a disaster or need in another country. With that, you could start a charity, a blog, a business, or write a book centered around that purpose and heart. Maybe your why is to invite people into love encounters with God. There are so many ways to accomplish that too—see? Most likely, you'll have many options for your whats and hopefully several large (and seemingly scary) goals to work towards! And, it's okay if these goals seem intimidating! Just be encouraged that someone needs this; someone needs you, and that in Christ, we can let His truths overcome our fears. Someone will find life, truth, identity, and encouragement from what you have to say. Everyone will do this a little differently, so don't compare, because your unique approach and experience will bring something to the table that this person perhaps hasn't heard before or may have really needed in that moment.

My best advice?  DON'T LET FEAR GET IN THE WAY.  Fear creates distance and cultivates disaster.

**Fear creates distance and cultivates disaster.**

Fear takes something God put in your heart, lies to you, and tells you that you're not good enough to do it. Kick that right in the butt because you ARE made for greatness. You are not made to live in worry, doubt, or anxiety but to create, inspire, and thrive out of your God-given identity. He tells you that you are more, you are worthy, and you are enough—so let's agree to listen to Him, not the enemy.

**Can you remember a time in your life when your heart "broke" for someone or something? Write it out here.**

_____

_____

_____

**Think back to this time, describe your emotions, your perspective, and who you were around.**

_____

_____

_____

By examining these moments where you felt so emotionally connected in something that was happening around you, you will be able to explore more of what God has put inside you. I have heard stories of friends that were on mission trips where they became so emotionally involved in one particular situation or area of brokenness that they encountered. This small moment of seeing things around them through their Father's eyes catalyzed their search for finding their why or their purpose. Take some time and think of a few moments where this has happened to you, and don't feel restricted! You can have more than one why, but just start by intentionally revisiting those moments until you begin to understand what God was teaching you through them.

As you explore this area, it can be scary! The enemy starts speaking negativity and death over this because he KNOWS it's powerful. If you hear, "You could never do that," "You could never change the world," or "This is stupid; you're not going to be able to accomplish anything," KEEP GOING. It seems counter-intuitive, but don't stop—whatever you do, don't stop. Lean into the Father's arms for strength and KEEP pursuing what He has put on your heart.

Once you've written them out, I want you to cross them out, and write next to them truths that come from the Father. This is something you can even do mentally or verbally as you walk this process out: identify the lie, call it out, and then speak truth over it!

**What is your why?**

_____

_____

_____

**What are some actionable steps you can take this week to further explore your why?**

_____

_____

_____

**What fears and lies are you experiencing right now regarding focusing on your why? It's important to call them out!**

_____

_____

_____

## BUILD YOURSELF

Through this journey of healthiness, you have to remember who you really are. Your foundation should always and only be found in the One who created you. This One is the whole reason for your existence and is the power behind learning yourself, loving yourself, and pursuing all your passions. So, write down declarations, spend time with your Papa asking questions, and ultimately, rest in the fact that He is yours and you are His. I encourage you to spend as much of your time as you can on this piece of the puzzle, building your foundation on Him. You may want success in the end, and that's not a bad thing, but remember that He came first, and He is the source of all good things. He wants to bless you and keep you. He wants to shine His face upon you and be gracious to you always (Numbers 6:24-25 ESV). He wants to bring peace, love, joy, and success to you, so rest in Him. Find time to love Him and love yourself, and then go after your dreams like a wildfire.

Always remember to let this journey of healthiness be yours. Don't compare or get frustrated if you don't think it's going the "right way," simply let it be yours. You are different than the next person because He made you unique in His image, so don't try to copy and paste someone else's image and progress with yours. Let this uniqueness flow out of you. He gave you a story to tell. Let this lead you into being intentional in relationships and intentional in chasing after your dreams and desires, always using all the creativity that was instilled in you from the very beginning.

**What is one thing God spoke to you while reading this chapter, and what steps are you going to take to engage Him more in this area?**

_____

_____

_____

_____

_____

_____

_____

_____

_____

_____

_____

# BE

"We were given bits and pieces of God's character, and designed with the ability to create, love, transform, reform, and restore."

# 5

# **B e**
*open*

Growing up, my dad used to say, "There are three sides to every story: your side, my side, and the truth." From an early age, this taught me the value of perspective. Simply because I experience something one way does not by any means translate to another person experiencing it the same way, and apart from both of those perspectives, there is what actually happened. This simple saying of my dad's instilled in me the foundational idea that other people matter; other people see situations differently than you, and you should approach every conversation and process events with grace and empathy for how someone else may be feeling or experiencing them, especially when you are hurt or upset.

To say it simply, there is always more. There is more to the story, more to the circumstance, more to their attitude, more to their anger, more to your hurt, more. There is more behind the scenes than we could ever imagine—always. I am not saying this to discredit where you are or tell you that what you are feeling or experiencing doesn't matter, but I want to inspire you to open your eyes a little. What you experience is a *piece* of the truth, but we always need to take time to learn what someone else is experiencing, too.

Relationships aren't one-sided systems. They are between two people, and therefore include all the emotions, hurt, brokenness, and experiences of each person. Relationships can be really powerful tools to display the characteristics of Christ, but first we have to have grace like Christ. Identity is so important here. For relationships to develop in a healthy way, there have to be healthy people making healthy choices. In every relationship, there comes a collision between your own identity and the identity of the other person. Through this collision, a great relationship can be established, but each person has to be willing to come to the table with open arms, ready to give grace, create hope, and understand that there is always more to the story, and there is always room for development.

## IT'S YOUR CHOICE

I have a friendship that, in the beginning, started out easy. This girl and I simply clicked right from the first day. We easily connected, had conversations that flowed, enjoyed the same things, had similar friend groups, all of it. This was a great beginning, but as time went on, we began to realize there was more that each of us was carrying than we thought. It took more than our easy connection to keep our friendship going because when tough times came and fights were had, we both had to choose the relationship above the frustrations. There comes a part in every relationship where a choice has to be made. Quite literally, you have to choose if you're going to stay connected to that person and if it is worth enough to you for the work that is going to go into it. Some things flow easy for a while, but a crossroad will come where you are faced with the decision to work or to walk. Thankfully, our example was Christ, and the beautiful choice He made to choose us continually was world-changing.

Part of successfully choosing another person is giving grace for the process that they are in. Similar to Christ's disposition with us, we need to be able to love the person where they are and believe for where they are going. In the same way, we must be willing to work through things when the going gets tough—and it will. A couple of years ago, I went through a really hard time. I walked through a lot of transition all at once, and not everyone in my life agreed with where I was going or what I was doing. Hard decisions had to be made by everyone to determine if the relationship was going to be chosen or not. I was also going through significant personal growth, and I can honestly admit that I wasn't in the healthiest state at the time. I wanted to be, but I didn't quite understand what healthiness looked like and how to represent it through all my decisions. Even though I had multiple people that walked away, I had so many that stayed and walked through it with me. I had so many people say, "I see the potential in this, and even though you aren't where you want to be right now, I trust the process, and I see the more that is available in your life." Those people showed me what choosing a relationship looked like. They partnered with me despite where I was, understood that I was in process, and walked out healing and healthiness with me in the middle of a turbulent time. They saw my true identity in Christ and said, "This is who you are, not your current struggles. Not your past." This is what it means to understand that everyone is in process. People are all at different stages, and nobody has it all right yet. If you are around someone that thinks they have absolutely everything figured out, run. A healthy person understands there is room for development and growth. So, give grace for the process. Give grace to those that are in the middle of transition and figuring life out, because we all are. Partnering with people in our relationships and choosing them even when it's not easy represents what love truly is. It's what Christ did; He chose you. He chose you when you didn't have it figured out yet. He chose you when you were deliberately not choosing Him. He chose you despite where you were, despite the choices you were making. He chose you no matter what because He loved you, and He saw the potential in you from day one.

This is represented in romantic relationships so clearly. Especially in marriage, the act of choosing your husband or wife each day is crucial. The initial connection may have been an easy click, but the follow through of a real relationship takes effort. The beauty in this is that through this effort, we can create healthy and fulfilling relationships that represent the love of Christ magnificently. He will use our relationships to show the world what life in Him is like, full of grace, love, peace, mercy, and understanding. When we focus on emulating these characteristics through our relationships with people, God can bring breakthrough for those who haven't experienced this on earth.

I don't know where you come from. I don't know what relationships you have had, or have, with other people. I don't know what hurts you've experienced or what pain you've been dealt in this messy journey called life. I don't know. There are exceptions in which choosing the other person in the relationship is not healthy for you and could potentially be detrimental to your well-being, so please understand that I am not at all advocating for a relationship that is abusive. Do not feel pressured to talk to, interact with, or walk through life with a person that doesn't respect you or your God-given identity. You don't have to choose the relationship; you can choose to walk away. If that is you, if you are in an unsafe situation, please take the necessary action that you need to get yourself safe, and then I encourage you to find counseling and people you trust to walk through the healing journey with you. Your first job is always to take care of yourself.

Part of healthiness is taking time to healthily view the other person—God's other child. This just means understanding that as people, we are all in process. We have all been broken; we've stumbled, and we've been hurt along the way. We are all on a journey with Him to work through those hurts, seeking the glory that will come out of them and the good for which He will use it. By simply opening our eyes to this, we are able to have healthy expectations of others and clearly communicate where we are and where we want the relationships to be.

## IT'S YOUR JOURNEY

I've been through stages in my journey, much as you probably have in yours. Maybe you're right in the beginning, right at the crossroads of choice with a person, or maybe you're working out the relationship after having already made your choice to put the effort in. Whether you've been doing this for years, searching and trying to find new ways to manage and assess the relationships you are involved in, or this is the beginning of your journey of intentionality, you will encounter different emotional stages along the way. You may go through phases where you feel angry, uncontrollably sad, experience bitterness beyond belief, or perhaps you've felt like you couldn't care less; the list of feelings go on and on. I have noticed in my life that these stages are cyclical, meaning one day I could be crying on my bed uncontrollably, and the next, I feel peace and like I can move on from it all without a tear. It's all part of the process on the journey to healing and healthiness.

Allow yourself to work through it all, because letting your emotions surface and be processed allows you to make a clear-headed decision on where to go next. Take a minute and pour out your hurts to God, giving Him all of your feelings and your frustrations. Write a letter to the person who hurt you, allowing yourself to get it all out – then rip it up after, creating a moment for you to partner with God in a prayer of blessing over them. Taking these steps to clear your heart and your mind puts you in a position to still give love, despite the hurt. Carrying out a relationship with someone that has hurt you can feel overwhelming, but the beauty of choosing someone is a reflection of Christ's love for them. This choice may result in a different type of relationship—it may lead to new boundaries being set, and this connection will more than likely look different than it did before. Follow the example of Christ by loving them where they are while still maintaining healthiness in your own life.

## IT'S YOUR PROCESS

Growing up, I've always bundled forgiveness and reconciliation together. I assumed when forgiveness was truly established, a relationship would return to an upgraded state of being, bringing us back together as if nothing had happened. I quickly learned through my childhood that simply forgiving does not automatically bring reconciliation with someone, because forgiveness is more about us than it is about the other person. Forgiveness is about "letting go and letting God." This cliché statement holds the truth that we don't have to carry things alone, that we have an almighty Papa who is there to help. His heart for relationships is immense, and His heart for you is even bigger. Learning how to lean on Him and walk through a healing process in forgiveness will bring greater outcomes than you could ever imagine.

One thing to always remember is that forgiveness usually comes before reconciliation. Sometimes reconciliation doesn't come right away, and sometimes the relationship is never the same, but just know that there is more available for both you, the other person, and your connection as you walk this out, and always, always remember that God uses all things for good. He can take ashes and create beauty.

**Forgiveness often comes before reconciliation.**

Let me clarify one thing: existing in healthiness doesn't mean never being sad. It doesn't mean never being angry. It doesn't mean never feeling the hurt you experienced because of someone else. It doesn't even mean being numb or never thinking about what happened. Healthiness means being able to rest in a place where you can understand that despite what happened, you are more, and there is more; where you can experience what happened and move forward with what you've gained. A place where you can look back and see the beauty in someone else, the beauty that God put there, even when their beauty may be hard to see through the veil of hurt and pain in your heart.

You are allowed to be sad, to be angry, to feel all the emotions that come as a result of adversity. You are allowed this for as long as you need. One truth I had to remember continually through this journey towards wholeness is that I am allowed to feel, that I am allowed to have emotions. It doesn't make me crazy, or weak, or "a woman" to cry about what happened. It is important that you allow yourself to feel those things. It is crucial to the healing process that you admit how the relationship made you feel, that you allow those emotions to surface, and that you process through them appropriately—opening a door for God to be with you in this.

You are allowed to feel it all, but don't set up camp there. The thing that hurt you sucked; it really did, but there is more to your life than that moment. We can find ourselves in the danger zone when we don't move on. This journey looks a little different for everyone, but the reality is that you have to pick yourself up a little day by day and move forward. You have to confront feelings of bitterness and sadness, assess how to handle them, and work step by step through them. Those relationships, decisions, and people don't define you; Christ does. So, pick yourself up, dust yourself off, and remember who you are and Whose you are. God made you, and God made them, and we are all in process.

## IT'S HIS IMAGE

I don't have any children yet, but I have experienced many family members and friends having them. It is such a unique experience to look at both parents and then look down at their newborn child who is a reflection of them. It is fun to figure out whose nose they have or whose chin they ended up with. Although some children look strikingly like one parent or the other, the reality is that each parent is represented partially in this being. Dad's side gets a part, and *mom's* side gets a part, and through each of their contributions, this child is formed.

It is the same with God and us. He presents Himself through every human being. Back in the documentation of creation, it says that we were made in the image and likeness of Him (Genesis 1:26-27). Each piece of us was knitted together in our mothers' wombs, all with Heavenly attributes of our Creator. We were given bits and pieces of His character, and we were designed with the ability to create, to love, to transform, to reform, and to restore.

Think about Adam and Eve. As a couple, united as one, they both brought different personalities and experiences to the table. Adam couldn't say he knew what it meant to be created from the rib of another human, but he could describe what being sculpted from the dirt was like, or what his experience was waking up and seeing his beautiful Eve was like, or the experience that was naming the animals. When God chose to instill features of Himself into each person, I believe He was building what would be a beautiful picture when people joined together in connection.

Think about a couple of people in your life and the Heavenly attributes that they embody. I have one friend, Melissa, who is simply full of love. She is kind, invites people in, listens to what's going on in my life, accepts me where I am, coaches and encourages me to where I am going, and so much more. The kind of love she shows me is an amazing glimpse of the kind of love that God has for all of us. I have another friend, my mom, who shows the greatest strength I have ever experienced in another human. She has been through so much in her life and has passed through resiliently and with her faith intact. She is strong, capable, hard-working, and a complete and total overcomer and champion. These two women are so different in that they each carry a different characteristic of God's so greatly. These characteristics are often brought out by circumstances, beliefs, relationships, and other aspects of life. These attributes shine brightly from their lives and give an encounter with God's heart to all with whom they interact.

**Who is one person in your life that you've learned something deeply impactful from?**

_____

_____

_____

**What attribute of God's character do you see in them?**

_____

_____

_____

I encourage you to do this for a couple of people; start to see the beauty with which God has surrounded you and start to see Him in more ways than you're used to!

I believe this picture doesn't stop here. Not only do we individually emulate pieces of God's character, but He does a similar thing through our connections with people. God's intention and design for us is to be in relationship with others, first exemplified through the declaration in Genesis that it wasn't good for man to be alone. We have always been created to be in community with other people. Relationships are a unique situation where two people come together, each with their own past, hurts, experiences, joys, successes, and personalities. If you look at every connection, each individual brings to the table a different version and glimpse of who God is. Relationships are an explosion of the present characteristics of God. For example, if my two friends were to sit in a room together and chat, God's love and strength would be so powerful in that moment. Each person brings a special glimpse in a unique way of these characteristics of God, and without that person in my life, I wouldn't be able to experience strength and love the same way that I am able to through those friends.

Think about a relationship in your life that is frustrating. God created every single person on this earth, and no matter what they have been through, what kind of life they lead, or what they have done to you, He purposefully placed glimpses of aspects of His character into that person. Recognizing this was a growing moment for me. Take a moment and ask God, "What is it that you see in that person? What is it that you love about them?" Reflect for a minute on a characteristic that they have that brought you into a deeper revelation of who He is. The next time you think of that person or are with them, try to focus on how God sees them. Filtering out our own experiences for a moment and being able to recognize the Christ in them will give us strength to show grace and love to them.

**What is one thing God spoke to you while reading this chapter, and what steps are you going to take to engage Him more in this area?**

_____

_____

_____

_____

_____

_____

_____

_____

_____

_____

_____

6

# **Be**
## *energized*

There are books upon books of guidelines outlining what a healthy relationship looks like. There are chapters that tell you how to set up boundaries, chapters that help you have the hard conversations, and chapters that help you walk through a healing process when a relationship is unhealthy. There are mentors and counselors in churches and organizations all over the world that will walk through this process with you and help you really identify what it looks like to cultivate health and wholeness in your life. To sit here and give you all the advice I have learned would take a long time, so I encourage you to seek out those resources if that is something you would find helpful. I am here to help you build a foundation, to realize that your identity is rooted in God, and all good and perfect things come from Him. I am here to help you understand your responsibility and roles in your life through understanding who Christ is and who He made you to be. I am here to help you learn to live purposefully and intentionally as you set out on this journey to cultivate the healthiest version of you.

Our ultimate example is always Christ, and when evaluating relationships for what is healthy or unhealthy, we always need to look to Him. We can't expect each connection to be perfect as we are imperfect, but understanding the values of Heaven can help us create boundaries and expectations for what our earthly relationships will look like. Remember as well that God's intention is to use community to be an earthly example of a Heavenly culture, so cultivating relationships that represent Christ's values is necessary in the follow-through.

## INVEST

Growing up, connecting with God was always presented to me in a very cookie-cutter way. People would say it was best if I had my quiet time first thing in the morning. If I read at least a chapter of the Bible per day, prayed a little as well, and then ended my time with thankfulness—this was the formula that I "had" to follow in order for my relationship with God to grow. Is that what God wants? None of those elements are bad, per se, but is that really what God's goal is for us through our time with Him? Is His heart for us to have a cookie-cutter lifestyle? Does He really want our time with Him to be a direct reflection of what everyone around us is doing? That's not the God I know, and as I grew deeper in my relationship with Him, I was able to see His joy in our individuality and uniqueness—both features He created us to have! I remember when I first embraced that I could write in my Bible, and you better believe that I immediately went and purchased all the pretty color pens I could. From then on, I started to add my personality and desires into how I spend time with God and how I study His word.

Since He created us all so different, doesn't it stand to reason that our interactions with Him would be equally as unique?

**What are some creative ways you can make your intimate time with the Father more reflective of your personality?**

_____

_____

_____

My time with God now is energizing, inviting, pure, and refreshing. My moments with my Father fill me with life for the rest of the day. Each day is like a building block for my faith, and as one brick is put on top of the other, I watch as my foundation gets stronger the more time I spend with Him. With a firm foundation, the less prone I am to topple over at a simple lie from the enemy. With a solid foundation, the more confident I am in my identity. With a stronger foundation, the more I have to give to others—more love, more kindness, and more peace—because the less I am focused on keeping myself together, the more I am focused on helping build others up.

There's a verse, Matthew 6:33, that tells us to seek first His kingdom and then He will take care of everything else (my paraphrase). When we root ourselves in Him and build our foundation upon the principles of Heaven, we don't have to worry about anything else. Seek first Heaven's values and all other things will be taken care of, all other things will be added to us. This isn't a magic formula to heal every relationship on the spot, but it does provide some guidance of where we can start and how we can understand what our responsibilities are in our relationships. Each week, do you invest time in building your foundation?

Having your own foundation is crucial because, as I am sure you have discovered, you can't control another person. You can't guarantee they will walk through healthy healing, and you can't always know if they are willing to choose you as much as you are to choose them. The difficulty of this can bring a lot of people to give up and stop trying. They think, "Well, if I can't really know that this will work out, I'm walking away," or, "I did all I could, it's up to them now. I'm done putting in effort." If I have learned one thing through this journey, it's that wholeness is a process. Having a healthy outlook and understanding of where you are and where you want to be is more crucial than trying to control the other person and shape the relationship into the mold you desire.

Always remembering to seek first the Kingdom, staying rooted in His values, and realizing God desires relationships to be used as a mirror of His characteristics will create a healthy and solid foundation to walk on. I have learned that this process is way less about the other person than it is about you. Christ calls you to hold steadfast to the truth of who He is and who you are, so your responsibility is yourself. How you act, react, communicate, and walk this out will reflect what values you are keeping in your heart. Once you establish what values Christ desires to instill in relationships, you have a list of what values Christ desires you to emulate, and when you walk hand-in-hand with Him daily, cultivating these elements in your life becomes a lot easier.

**What is one thing God spoke to you while reading this chapter, and what steps are you going to take to engage Him more in this area?**

_____

_____

_____

_____

_____

_____

_____

_____

_____

_____

_____

# 7

# **Be**
*intentional*

As you begin to process through your relationships, I encourage you to make a list of Heavenly values. As you search through the Bible, what are values of Kingdom-minded relationships that you see? Things like love, joy, peace, patience, kindness, goodness, faithfulness, gentleness, and self-control, which are fruits of the Spirit that manifest themselves when Christ is in the middle of something (Galatians 5:22-23). Also, spend some time exploring your personal relationship with Christ, asking Him what values are important to Him in relationships. Work on cultivating this list and using it as a reference for your connections, allowing it to be a starting place for you to build intentional relationships.

As I walk through some of my personal discoveries about His values in my life, I have to keep myself in check. It is so easy to learn these things and then immediately turn around and point a finger at another person saying, "You aren't doing this right. You're not being Christ-like. You're not respecting me. You're not carrying these values in your life and into our relationship," and on and on and on. The reality is that the act of accusing isn't Christ-like either. You have to walk forward realizing that as much as these are guidelines for what healthy connection with others look like, they are even more guidelines for your responsibilities in relationships. If a relationship must have unconditional love, it is your responsibility to bring it, if it needs more grace, it is your responsibility to provide it, and if it requires forgiveness, it is your responsibility to give it. There's more and more that will require you to look inward to your heart as you walk this out.

## COMMUNICATION

If you are married, or hope to be married one day, you will need to learn the importance of open communication. In my experience, the number one response I have gotten from couples when reflecting on what led to success in their marriage is: "communication, communication, communication." This seemed so abstract to me before, and as Jeffrey and I walked through marriage counseling and mentorship, this value was always regarded with such a high priority. To be honest with you for a minute, I sincerely thought that the key having a great marriage meant ALWAYS telling Jeffrey how I felt when I felt it. I constantly, even in a nice way, was telling him where I was at emotionally, spiritually, and physically. The significance I placed on this value wasn't bad, it was simply misdirected and misunderstood.

Healthy communication is more than simply telling someone the first thing that comes to your mind when you think it. It is about being concise, clear, and completely processing something before we say it. A maturity step I had to take was realizing that processing things internally was necessary first before I went out and shared them with Jeffrey. I don't have to share everything with him, but I need to make it a priority to keep our lines of communication open so that when there are things we need to process together or there are issues that I find necessary to discuss with him, there is space for it. I've learned that the more words you say, the less value your words have. If I am constantly oversharing my emotions and processes, he will naturally take me less seriously when I really am needing to communicate deep things with him. Learning discernment of what to share and what not to share is important in any relationship.

A healthy relationship should be an environment where your voice can always be heard, and your emotions can always be welcomed. We as humans need to be able to be honest and vulnerable, so we should partner with people who help cultivate a climate that provides this. In turn, we need to be quick to listen, slow to speak, and slow to become angry (James 1:19) when things are brought to us by the other person. Through emulating these Heavenly characteristics, we will be able to access healthy communication in times of disarray.

Make communication a priority. As we walk through healthy boundaries and expectations, keep the importance of this in mind. Reading through this book to gain information and insight is step one; learning how to carry these principles through to your own life and then sharing them in your relationships is step two.

**Are there some feelings you have towards a relationship that you haven't communicated well enough?**

_____

_____

_____

**What does God say about communication?**

_____

_____

_____

HINT: Start by looking in James 1, Ephesians 4, and Proverbs 15

## BOUNDARIES

Boundaries are another essential part to healthy relationships. Have you ever heard the phrase, "With great power comes great responsibility"? Dispute exists to who originally said it, but this age-old phrase has great truth buried in it. God did not create us, fill us with power and authority, then sit back and delight in us going to our own devices. He has created us in His image, which does mean we have inherent worth, power, creativity, and authority, but with this great power comes great responsibility. One aspect of responsibility is creating and setting boundaries in our connections with others. I used to think that boundaries were negative—walls put up to keep bad things out. However, just like rules created for the safety of a child (not crossing the street before looking both ways), boundaries are set up to protect. Each healthy relationship needs defined boundaries for it to survive, and the best way to go about this is to establish them using clear communication (see how it all connects?).

One example in my life of a healthy boundary was created in my marriage. When we first got married, we specifically created a boundary that during fights (or "discussions" as I like to call them), we can't leave the house. By establishing this early on, we are able to help cultivate a safe space to communicate when we are emotionally overwhelmed. By knowing that I won't leave Jeffrey, and Jeffrey won't leave me, we are able to protect our hearts during a fragile time.

There are probably hundreds more examples I could give of healthy boundaries to set up in relationships: anything from establishing what you'd like to be called by a coworker to communicating what times of the day you will answer your texts, we can use communication to set ourselves up for success in our connections with others.

Take time to sit down and really think through where you are comfortable and uncomfortable, happy and unhappy in your current relationships. It doesn't need to be as much of a "business deal" as it sounds right now, but knowing where you stand and what you want is important to creating connections that emulates Heavenly values.

## HONESTY

I have one friendship that was built on unspoken expectations. I hadn't learned at the point of this relationship forming to communicate what I needed, and to be honest, I don't even really think I knew what I wanted. This woman and I had been friends for quite a few years when all of a sudden, the pressure of unspoken expectation and failed realization collided into a period of three months where we didn't speak. I am willing to admit that after all of that time, she was the one who first reached out, and after setting a date and time to talk, the anxiety set in for the upcoming conversation. Walking into Starbucks that day was nerve-wracking to say the least. With all the knots in my stomach, and the notes in my phone, I felt as prepared as I could be for something like this. Over the next several hours, we took time to share our frustrations and our hurts that came out of the last several years of friendship. Then, we shared our desires and together, set expectations for the future of our relationship. The vulnerability it took for both of us to be honest with each other was immense as we talked through things we'd buried for so long. Despite the fact that the baristas probably thought we were crazy with all of our tears and all of our refills, the outcome of this open communication was a stronger friendship than we've ever had.

As you walk through relationships, you will discover that you have more internal expectations than you realized, and giving yourself time to reflect and communicate them is important. You could have expectations of how much time you will spend together, how often you will communicate, what types of activities you will do together, or how they will pay attention to you and in what way, and so much more.

I quickly realized in the beginning of my marriage that I had assumed that Jeffrey would put dirty clothes in a dirty laundry basket at the end of each day. As silly as this is, when reality didn't line up with my expectation, I was upset. After bottling all the "upset" up until it overflowed in a "discussion," I quickly realized that I had never communicated this assumption to my husband. He didn't realize that I wanted him to do this, and although simple communication didn't fix it all, it opened up the door for a conversation of compromise through healthy communication.

**What is one thing God spoke to you while reading this chapter, and what steps are you going to take to engage Him more in this area?**

_____

_____

_____

_____

_____

# 8

# Be
*willing*

Allow yourself space and time to express your voice on this journey. Healthiness and establishing boundaries doesn't come without intentional work, but it is so worth it. Don't be shy or self-conscious that you're asking for too much. The truth is, when these patterns are established early on through clear communication, the redefinition processes in the future go smoother, because there is already an established environment for communication present. Remember, it's not too late for those relationships that have been around for a while either. Some of the largest redefinitions I have gone through were in lifelong relationships. When you are in process, growing and learning in your life, you are bound to hit points with each connection with another person you have where you begin to redefine it. It's not bad or selfish, it's a natural part of the cycle. By choosing to continue a relationship with someone, you are taking on the responsibility of continually communicating with them where you are and where you would like to see the relationship go.

We aren't made to live in unhealthy, incomplete relationships. We are called to be more, to do more, and to create more. This world gives us access to limited resources, and through the unlimited resources and support of Heaven, we can show the world what healthy looks like, and ultimately show the world what Heaven looks like. This takes action—one of the hardest steps in the process. Knowing something is simple but doing something about it takes courage, confidence, and trust. Be encouraged that I am doing this alongside you, coaching and cheering you on—and the Holy Spirit is here to partner with you and see you through this journey. You may have to take some hard steps as you walk through this book and as you begin to evaluate changes in your life, but you can do it! I encourage you to find someone that can walk through this with you. Find someone who understands these values, understands you, and understands these relationships and the areas in which you are seeking change. Look for a person you can trust that will help guide you as you walk through messy situations, and ultimately, who can believe for the *more* that Christ put in you, the *more* that we are called to, and the *more* that Christ has for you in each and every one of your relationships.

## BE GRACIOUS

There are going to be moments in life where other people need a little room to grow; where people around you need you to understand that they are in process too. Here's my advice: always remember to give grace. Christ loves you where you are and walks through life with you to take you where you are going. Every person on this earth is in process, which means every relationship is also in process. There may be current connections with others that are extremely unhealthy in your life or in which you are needing to communicate boundaries and expectations. You need to always remember to give grace. Whether you decide that it is best to walk away from that toxic environment or stay and work through it, it is important to understand the process is as real as the struggle. These outcomes won't always be realized in 24 hours so have patience. The other person is working through stuff as well. Overall, this is a growing process for both of you, and although it might not be easy, it will be worth it.

The reality is that the healthier you are inside, the stronger your relationships will be. It also means your current relationships may require redefinition. Use this book as a launching pad to cultivate wholeness in your life out of your God-given identity. Christ has planned more than you could imagine for you, so collaborate with Him in everything. Remember that His heart is always restoration and redemption, and by partnering with Him, we can access the unlimited resources of Heaven and bring them down to earth—creating world-changing outcomes in our life.

## BE INTENTIONAL

I almost called this section "Evaluating Relationships," but as I began to write it out, I realized that building intentional relationships is even more important than evaluating your relationships. Intentional relationships are those that you invest into purposefully, those that you find valuable enough to give your time, your money, your attention, your advice, your emotion, etc.

One silly, yet helpful, example: right after my husband and I got married, we were faced with the test of choosing a church. I was the kind of girl that had only gone to one or two churches my entire life. My family would choose a church and stay and invest, and the only time I can think of us changing churches was when we moved to a whole new city and the old church was over an hour away (because when it was still exactly an hour away, we went). Anyway, as we discussed what we were going to do, we decided to both leave our respective churches and together, as a couple, search for a new one that fit both of our preferences and comforts.

One of the large conversations we had in the midst of this was the emotions that came with leaving a church we each had been at for a while. I had never experienced what it was like, so I was simply giddy and excited for new opportunities. Jeffrey, however, had been through the game of having to leave churches and move forward one-too-many times. He opened up about the frustration with how many relationships you lose when you move churches. You think those connections are firmly established, but you quickly learn that the largest factor keeping them together was the common ground of that church (kind of like school and all those "bestest friends" you never saw again). Anyway, after that evaluation, he sort-of made a mental list of all the relationships that he was going to intentionally keep going once he left the church he was currently attending. He spent time talking to them, hanging out with them, going to dinner with them, and overall, he carried on the relationships intentionally instead of letting that large change interrupt and eventually destroy them.

It's the same way with your relationships in life. Be intentional. Choose the people that you really do want in your life and show them that you do. Keep relationships going. Call them once a week or once every other week. Invite them to dinner. This doesn't mean they have to be your new best friend that you go to for everything; it just means being intentional enough to maintain the connection you have and not letting circumstances ruin it.

I want you to walk through these next questions with one of the closest relationships in your life. Focus on building intentionality while you're filling this out.

**What is this person's name and how did you meet them?**

_____

_____

_____

**How often do you communicate or interact with this person?**

_____

_____

_____

**Are there any areas you feel are lacking in this relationship?**

_____

_____

_____

**Have you communicated your feelings to the other person?**

_____

_____

_____

**What are 3 steps you can take this week to be more intentional in this relationship? (This could be making a point to call, to visit them, to get them a gift, to have a heart-to-heart conversation, etc.)**

1. _____

_____

**2.**

_____

_____

**3.**

_____

_____

## BE TEACHABLE

Let me preface here that I am no pro, nor do I claim to be. I've learned most of what has made Jeffrey and I successful from other people who are older, wiser, and married much longer. However, there are a few things that I learned on my own that I think are important as well. Either way, these are my favorite pieces of advice to you when building intentional relationships.

I had a teacher in high school that was AMAZING. You ever have that one teacher that knew the perfect balance of encouragement and challenge? Who took the time to know you personally and helped walk you through not only the curriculum, but life? I had this teacher for several years and for several different classes in school—let's call her Mrs. Style, and she LOVED teaching. You could tell she loved relationships, seeing students excited, and being a partner on their journey of learning and knowledge, she loved it all.

She was great, but there was one particular thing she did that really stood out, and no other teacher ever did with me. She was a science and mathematics teacher, so she taught on subjects that were not always well-received or well-understood. However, simply teaching it and maybe personally coaching the students wasn't going to be fit for her classroom, so every single year, at the beginning of her classes, she would give a "Learning Styles Test." Have you ever taken one of these? They are basically these tests where you answer all kinds of questions about your personality and the way you prefer to receive and take in information. At the end, it spits out this answer of what learning styles you most cling to. There are seven in all, but there are four that relate to the senses of your body.

- Visual (spatial)
- Aural (auditory-musical)
- Verbal (linguistic)
- Physical (kinesthetic)

These results reveal how you learn best (they remind me of the five love languages, but for school). Through this experience, Mrs. Style would learn whether each of her students learned through visual aids, by hearing the content, by speaking the content, or by interacting with the content (kinesthetic). She would take these results and be sure to mix up the styles of the lessons she taught, as well as have a better knowledge base of how to help a student who may have been struggling.

After doing this every year for four years, it stuck with me. Recently, it surfaced in a situation and reminded me of how life-changing this could be when applied to relationships.

My husband and I, at the point of me writing this, have been married just over a year. When you get married, you get to experience your partner in different scenarios or situations than you may have seen them before. One of these scenarios for me was church. Although throughout dating and engagement Jeffrey and I attended church together a few times, we didn't consistently go together because we both worked at our respective churches. Because of that, marriage was a new experience of getting to worship and learn together.

Let me insert this before we go on, Jeffrey is really smart. Like I used to think I was smart, but he is super smart. He has a knack for not only picking up like a billion useless facts and spitting them out at parties, but he also just has the logistical brain to know how things work and function. If he doesn't, he goes and learns. It makes sense that he is in the IT world for sure.

Okay so back to church. Since we have been married, let's say about 60 weeks, we have gone to church together maybe about 55 times. In addition, we have done some different discipleship or school-based learning classes together as well. So, let's just say that 70 times in the last year, we have sat together in these environments in churches together. To be totally transparent, almost all 70 of those times, I have been so frustrated with him. He helps run various functions of the church, so we are not always right next to each other during the services, and sometimes I will look over at him and he seems COMPLETELY disinterested. COMPLETELY. Guys, growing up, that was not allowed. You paid attention in church (or at least pretended like you were!)

As the weeks went by, and all my frustration was building, I finally got to a breaking point. I had to figure this out because although I had kind of brought it up to him before, I had never had a real conversation with him about it. So, after a class one night, I was at the end of my rope. *'My husband, not paying attention in* church.

*How does that make me look? Does he even care about Jesus? Does he even like Him? Does he even care about learning? Oh, you know what, he probably just thinks he's too smart for this. No good..."* I won't lie, these are some of the thoughts that went through my head, and in that moment, after that class, I was ready to explode. And that was when I heard God say, *"Miranda, just ask him."* Um... excuse me God... ask him? No no no no no, *I already know. He's not paying attention... "* Miranda, just ask him."

So, I did. We got home that night, and I brought it up. I told him what I was observing, and as a result the assumption (a.k.a. judgment) I was making, and we talked about it. Come to find out, those environments are really hard for him to learn in. He is a kinesthetic and visual learner, so by simply hearing, reading, or writing, he has a really hard time focusing. Once I heard that, I felt so bad. I had looked at him and basically thought, "You don't act like me..." and made all these rash judgments. I concluded that because I learn best a certain way, he should learn best in the same way.

After all of this, we had a long conversation about the environments he does learn best in. I learned something about him that day that I had never really taken the time to know before, and in the end, we were both much happier because of our conversation. In turn, I learned that I can't make assumptions before asking questions, and I also learned how important it is to know the people around you (friends, spouses, significant others, family, etc.) so you don't end up assuming things based on misinformation.

All of that to say, learn more about those you are in relationship with. Learn their love languages. Or their favorite snack. Or their learning styles. You'll be surprised what asking questions before making assumptions creates in your connection.

## BE FIRST

This one is the hardest for me, for sure. Other ways to say this are "be the bigger person" and "forgive first." However you say it, the concept is this: you act, despite what they do.

**You act, despite what they do.**

Remember the story in the last section? Well, the next week when we were in class, Jeffrey made a point to come over, sit next to me with his notebook, and try. His learning style didn't change between the week before and then, but he saw that it was important to me, and he made an effort. It meant so much to look over and see this and to know that our conversation really went deeper than just a simple talk on a Tuesday night.

Are you currently in a fight with someone? Is there something that frustrates you beyond belief? Maybe they don't take out the trash regularly, or they don't call you as often as you'd like, or it seems as though you ALWAYS pick up the bill, and you don't feel as though they contribute. You may have mentioned this to them, in kindness, or perhaps, not in the nicest way. If you've made a rude remark, don't worry, I've been there too. I've been in the moments with the low comments, the bitter words, the side glances... all of it. I've been in the moments where you feel like they don't understand you, they don't care about you, and they don't even want to try—all concluded from one moment of disappointment or hurt. I've been in those arguments where I've yelled one thing "they" don't do, and "they've" brought up something I didn't do, and the cycle of missed expectations is never-ending.

My advice to you? Be first.

Be kind first. Be forgiving first. Be encouraging first. Be the first to try to understand and move forward. Be the first to love. Really, really love. Not conditional love, where they get to experience your love when they follow the expectations you have in your head of the things they should be doing and contributing in your relationship. No. That isn't the example of love that Christ gave, and it isn't the example of love that we should be emulating. Be the first to give the hug and kiss when they come in the door. Be the first to ask how their day was. Be the first to serve, to love, and to encourage. Be the first.

One of the hard parts to understand is that you should do this even when they don't respond with the same actions. This is exactly what I mean by *"you act, despite what they do."* It doesn't matter how they act; what matters is how you act. This is part of being intentional and preserving commitment, no matter the environment. Your job isn't to always be reminding someone else what they have to do or how they have to change. Your job (and mine) is to encourage, to help, to understand, and to love— even when the other person is still growing. Be the first to set the environment of unconditional love and encouragement and watch the powerful changes that begin to happen in your life.

## BE AWARE

Healthy relationships reflect God's character in a new way. When we intentionally are first, we take our relationships to a new level of intimacy, vulnerability, acceptance, love, hope, and expectation than before. In an ideal situation, characteristics of God should be shining so brightly out of the connections you have with others that they would bring people into a whole new encounter with God.

As I mentioned previously, every single person was made in the image of God. This pattern didn't end with Adam and Eve, it carried on through generations, and when we look around, we can see the mural of beauty that He has painted on this world. Each one of us carries different aspects of Him. Imagine the explosion when two people join together. When you and your friend get together, what do they bring out in you and what do you bring out in them? What outcomes do you have together that bring love and encouragement to others?

Let's look at our own experiences in relationships and begin, on a small scale, to evaluate each one.

**To start, I want you to write down the top 5 people you spend the most time with.**

**1.**
_____

**2.**
_____

**3.**
_____

**4.**
_____

**5.**
_____

Great, now I want you to write one word next to their name—one characteristic of them that you greatly admire. This could be their hope, encouragement, perseverance, love, ability to dream, passion, anything. Write one positive word that comes to your mind about this person. What do they bring to your life in a significant way?

It is so important when walking through this process of relationships that we take time to recognize admirable qualities in people. Sometimes, in the midst of redefinition, it can be so difficult to see any good in someone. I am not in your situation, and I cannot attest or even begin to sympathize with some of the things you may have gone through. I am not asking that you write off all the bad and hurt this person may have caused and cover it with this one great characteristic (which in your opinion, may be their only one). However, in all my experiences, healing cannot happen until you can look back and pull out what God has done through it. Being able to look at that person and say, "I know you hurt me, but you are just as in process as I am. As we all walk through this journey, it isn't easy, and I forgive you. In addition, I greatly admire your _____ that you've always shown...", takes you to new places in the healing process.

Alright, do you have your list done? I am so proud of you! Being able to open up and find the good in someone is exactly what Jesus did. No matter what anyone did to Him or who He came across, He was able to look and see the good instilled in them from their very creation, see the potential in their lives, and out of that healthy place, He cultivated healthy relationships.

# BE IMITATE-ABLE

Growing up in church, I heard many pastors say that when we were living a life filled with Jesus, people would look at us and say, "They have something; I want that." Do you remember the stories in the Bible of the crowds following Jesus? They looked at Him, saw something enticing, and followed. They needed to know what was happening because they heard from friends and family of this mysterious man who demonstrated a new way of life, an attractive way of life.

I love looking into Jesus's life and the patterns that He expressed to learn more about who we are called to be on this earth. Being an example that demonstrates the attractiveness of living "in Christ" is a pretty hefty life goal, but it's through small changes and everyday choices that we cultivate and build a life that shows people all that is offered to them in the Kingdom.

This all starts with realizing your identity and letting those truths flow into every area of your life. We will spark change around us as we learn what healthy looks like and better build our life with Heavenly views of ourselves and others. Things such as anxiety, fear, anger, pettiness, jealousy, and hatred are just a few of the characteristics that subside when we begin to see ourselves and others like Christ does. When we realize who we were made to be and recognize that others were made in His image as well, the way that we live out our relationships looks different from the values of culture around us. This enticingly healthy perspective and lifestyle will bring others into an experience with Christ that their heart longs for and so desperately needs. A culture of acceptance, unconditional love, peace, joy, grace, and mercy is one that people around you need –and it starts with you.

God has a plan that He desires to accomplish on this earth. I fully believe that in one instant, He could carry out His desires here—because He is that powerful. However, God chose us to accomplish His purpose through. Even from the beginning with the story of Adam and Eve, humans were part of God's plan; creation is part of God's story. I love realizing this and then letting the empowerment from Christ set in. He chose me. He chose you. He has a specific purpose for our lives, and our job is to live through who He has called us to be. Our job is to demonstrate Kingdom values to the culture around us, and it all starts with knowing who you are and Whose you are.

**What is one thing God spoke to you while reading this chapter, and what steps are you going to take to engage Him more in this area?**

_____

_____

_____

_____

_____

_____

# EMBRACE

*"You aren't broken. You might be a little cracked, but your story isn't over yet because you can be restored."*

# 9

# Embrace
*the healing*

This world is messy, and this life is full of ups and downs. Even in just my 23 years, I have experienced some of the highest highs and the lowest lows. From the day I was born, through graduations, to my wedding day, to the first time I led worship, and all the memories in between, I have experienced so much, both good and bad. I have been broken and crying, been joyful and dancing. I have met so many people, had so many relationships, left so many relationships, and chased after moments and people that I thought would give me something more.

One thing that keeps me going is that I was made for more. This world was created for more. God didn't make us simply to lose us and leave us. He didn't create us so He could walk away as soon as we screwed up. He is here for it all—He's not distant, He's in it.

**He's not distant, He's in it.**

God is here in the hurts and frustrations as much as He is here in all the joy and jubilations. Through it all, we have Him, and He created us for so much more. He wants us to experience the desires of our hearts and the joys of living out our dreams. He wants us to experience the fullness of wholeness and restoration. He wants us to get to know Him better so we can understand who He really is and carry others into this love encounter with Him.

Take time to get to know Him. In the midst of all you are going through, lean on Him, hold His hand, and let Him walk alongside you. Let Him into that hurt and pain, share it with Him. Let Him come in and start to fill those broken cracks, let Him restore.

It helps to look back at the faithful patterns of God and the fulfilled promises you've seen in your life. I find that the follow-through of God in the past often catalyzes the hope I have for my current situation, as well as my future. Although it may take some time of reflection, there are so many moments in your past when God walked in right when you needed Him. The truth is: He doesn't leave you. He won't forsake you. He is always there, even when you can't feel or sense Him. When looking over the times in our life where God came through for us, some are more obvious than others. Maybe financial provision came right when you needed it, or maybe a situation turned around for the better unexpectedly. God is always looking for ways to show His love to us, because we are His kids.

**Share one of the most memorable moments that God has been there for you. Describe it in detail below.**

_____

_____

_____

_____

_____

_____

During Biblical times, the potter in the town was a big deal. Tupperware didn't exist, so if you ever wanted storage containers, or bowls, or plates, or cups, you went to the potter. This left a lot of pressure on the potter to fill this need in the community. Despite all his hard work to make something of quality that wouldn't break and would sustain weathering, occasionally the pieces he made would crack and this would add to the load of the potter. Now the piece he had previously made would be useless, and he would be stuck making twice as much pottery as he threw his work of broken art in the trash.

The problem escalated until the potter couldn't handle it

anymore—a solution was needed. What if the broken pottery could be fixed? What if, instead of throwing it out, it could be somehow mended and restored back to its original integrity? Through trial and error, the potter discovered by using a tick off of a bull or a cow, the cracks could be repaired. All they had to do was find the tick, crush it, and mix the blood with new clay. Then, the potter would re-fire the broken piece of pottery, and when it came out, it was good as new. The crack was filled, and you could never tell it almost had to be thrown out!

When I heard this story, I was so encouraged (by everything except the blood and tick part; that kind of grossed me out).

You aren't broken. You might be a little cracked, but your story isn't over yet because you can be restored. This is what Jesus did for us, a little blood mixed with some new creation and we are good as new. Now when God sees us, He doesn't see the old, broken, cracked piece that we once were, but the new, restored, shiny piece that He created us to be.

**You aren't broken.**

He wants you to let Him fill those cracks. He wants you to open your heart, so He can come in, and with some of His blood and some new clay, restore what was once broken to make it good as new, maybe even better and stronger than before. Jesus will restore you; you just have to let Him.

*"But now, O LORD, you are our Father; we are the clay, and you are our potter; we are all the work of your hand."*
*Isaiah 64:8 (ESV)*

**What is one thing God spoke to you while reading this chapter, and what steps are you going to take to engage Him more in this area?**

_____

_____

_____

_____

_____

_____

_____

_____

_____

_____

_____

# 10

# Embrace
*the process*

Let me be real with you. Some days are going to suck. This world isn't perfect, and neither is your life. Whether you are walking through a really messy relationship or you are just trying to figure out how to love yourself, it won't feel glorious every day. I can't take the pain or uncertainty away, but I can encourage you a bit because I have been there. I've walked through seasons where I've felt God physically next to me and seasons where I had no clue where to even look for Him.

This book is intended to show you the truth behind who you are. It is here to give you encouragement straight from the Father, to bring you back into sweet communion with Him in His presence, and to spur you on to find Him in the midst of what is going on. God's heart is meant to be represented through relationships, and Jesus desires healthiness in all of our interactions. This leads me to believe that healthy relationships are one of the best ways to reflect the character of God in our daily lives. By realizing who we are and learning to love people like Jesus did, we can bring light and life to a world that needs it—to a world that desperately needs to see who God truly is.

I can't promise every day will be easy, or even that tomorrow will be easier than today was, but I can encourage you to embrace the process. Life can't be absolutely perfect all of the time, but it can absolutely be hope-filled every day. This is what Jesus offers us—hope. He didn't come to condemn and shame and judge, He came to offer life, restoration, relationship, and hope. In Him, there is more. In Him, there is life. Through Jesus, Heaven came to earth and wholeness and restoration touched the soil we walk on, impacted the ancestors we've read about. Have faith. Give love. Receive love. Drive yourself toward greatness and hold His hand the entire time, knowing full well He has your back, and He can be trusted. **He will restore**—repeat it, repeat it, repeat it—until you believe it.

## STEPS FOR SUCCESS

Embrace the process, move through it, and most importantly, don't set up camp in it. You are more, there is more, and some of these helpful tips below might help you find routines that will make this process a little easier. Tape these on your wall, write them down, put up a post-it note, put them in your phone—whatever you have to do to remember them.

### ONE – think positive thoughts.

Daily. For the same reasons that declarations are so powerful, your thoughts become your realities. Even if you don't feel it, start to say it, start to think it, and eventually you will start to believe it.

Even if your instinct is to think, "Oh my, this person is the rudest, meanest, harshest person in the world, and this relationship will never be anything ever again," stop yourself and think, "There are good things about this person, this can be restored (or it's okay that this ended) ...", etc.

Another aspect of this is in your dreams and desires. God wants to give you the desires of your heart (Psalm 37:4). As His child, He delights in pouring out gifts to you, and love to watch you enjoy Him. I remember reading a quote once, whose authorship is attributed to Henry Ford, that said, "Whether you believe you can do a thing or not, you are right."[1] This holds so much truth—truth that there really is something to positive thinking. I encourage you to talk with God about what it is you want, and run after your dreams with your whole heart. If you are thinking the entire time, "I won't be able to accomplish this," you probably won't. Change the way you think.

**TWO – take time for yourself.**

In the midst of all the craziness you are going through, you need time for yourself. Remember how the only person you can control is yourself? Take time to read, pray, meditate, sit quietly, watch a movie, relax, get your nails done—whatever it is. Take time to be purposefully alone and do something you love. Reconnect with who you are and who He made you to be so out of that, you can start to live life how He intended. Building up all the emotions and distancing yourself from... well, yourself, is not ever the healthy solution. At the end of the day, you are left with you, so learn to love yourself.

## THREE – take things in stride.

LITERALLY everyone and their mother and their brother and their aunt's cousin's cat are going to have an opinion on what is happening in your life. Unfortunately, you can't stop that. Your responsibility in those moments is your reaction. You can be polite and respectful through these interactions and still walk away controlling their volume knob in your head. They can have advice or opinions, but you don't have to carry them. You are free to take what they've said and evaluate it against what God says—then keep hold of the truth and dispose of the lie.

## FOUR – find people to do this with.

Being open and being vulnerable about your hurts and your past and your process isn't always going to be easy. Find safe, healthy people, to process life with. Have conversations, let the tears out, and allow yourself to be built up in the best way by them. Learn to trust again. Even though other relationships may have let you down, the best thing you can do is pick yourself up and trust again. Don't build up walls. It isn't healthy. Don't push those who really love you away. That isn't healthy. Find people you can trust and be real with about it all—the good parts, the bad parts, the hard parts, and all the other parts in between.

## FIVE - have grace with yourself.

You're not required to be perfect or to handle things the "right" way (whatever that is). Give yourself a little grace! Life isn't always easy, and this journey of healthiness in relationships and learning to love myself hasn't always gone smoothly or quickly.

This isn't something that can be worked through in a day, or even a week. Give yourself grace, give yourself time, know that you aren't wrong or weak or unworthy for taking so long or taking too short of a time—there isn't a "right way" to do this or a "right time" to do this in.

## THERE IS MORE

Do you know that song "Reckless Love" by Cory Asbury? This song came out and exploded, not only because it's a good tune and musically pleasing to the ears, but because it has an amazing message. Have you ever stopped to think about the real, reckless, love of God? About the unconditional, never-ending, never-leaving, never-changing love of God? I remember the moment that this truth really hit me. I was listening to the song, and in an instant, God showed me that it didn't matter the love I was shown, the love churches showed me, the love boyfriends or friends had tried to show me. It didn't matter because these were all incomplete versions of real love, and He was nothing like that. His love doesn't change or run away in the face of sin or trouble. His love never condemns or shames. His love never once looked at me and said, "Sorry, you're not good enough." He simply loves because I am, because I exist, because I am His daughter, and I am exactly how He created me to be.

This is what makes it reckless. It's abnormal, and people don't love this way. It's not "normal" to throw your all into a relationship, even when the other person isn't healthy or doesn't understand your love yet. It's not "normal" to love despite obstacles, despite challenges. It's not "normal" to chase us down and break down every wall—it's against the norm, so it's considered reckless. God would do *anything* for you, anything at all without even a thought of what others will think. He loves you that much.

The feeling is kind of like drinking a warm drink. My favorite thing to do on cold, rainy days, is to curl up with a tea, coffee, or hot cocoa and simply relax. Imagine the first sip as the hot liquid coats your throat and fills your insides. You can almost feel it spread throughout your entire body as the warmth expands and you just feel... comfort. God's love is like that liquid. It fills us up, no matter our past, our mistakes, our frustrations, anything. It fills us up despite our family, our friends, or any of the broken relationships we have and wish we didn't have. It fills us up even though we yelled at our spouses. It fills us up even though we cussed at those drivers. It fills us up, and it comforts. It loves us through and through.

This truth is so crucial to understanding identity, because from this fact, all else stems. If you understand that God loves you unconditionally, you can not only begin to understand what unconditionally loving yourself looks like, but also it means to show love to others. Others need to experience the love of God. They need a glimpse of that through you. and this is the best thing you can give any relationship you are in. They sinned? Love covers all. They are rude? Love covers all. They didn't make a choice that you would have made? Love covers all. They look different from you? Love covers all. They act different than how you (or God) thinks they should act? Love. Covers. All.

All is an inclusive word. It doesn't exclude because of action or circumstance or personality or shortcomings. It doesn't exclude because of weaknesses, and it doesn't include more because of strength. Love simply covers all because God is love, and God is perfect.

Understanding that everyone in our lives desperately needs this truth is so important. Imagine if His love infiltrated the earth in a powerful way. Imagine if all the things you are realizing or have realized before about God's love influenced how people acted, how people treated one another, or how people responded to Christ. God could definitely come down from Heaven right now and speak these words. He could remind us of the truths of His love, or He could use you. He could use the relationship and the story that you have with that person to show them His love. He could use this truth to not only grow you one step closer to Him but also to lead others into that experience and encounter with His love as well.

First, you have to be willing. Willing to really *love*. To love despite shortcomings and mistakes. To love despite differences or uncomfortable situations. You have to be willing to be the example. You have to truly understand what unconditional means. You have to step into these uncomfortable environments and learn more and more what this reckless love of God thing really looks like.

Second, you have to embrace that this is part of the process. Part of the process of restoration, healing, and wholeness is love. In fact, it is the process. If you begin to really dive in to what Jesus looks like, to what He values, what He accomplished, what He really wanted to do by coming to Earth, then you will see that love was at the hot-lava center of it. Love was right there at the core from which everything flowed out. This revelation of love both then and now is the exploding volcano that changes people's lives. This revelation is the giant wave that overtakes and comforts all in one. This is the truth that we all must seek to understand above anything else. If John 3:16 holds true, and we wholeheartedly believe "God so loved the world" and that led

Him to do all that He did (including sending His Son), then we must make this a priority in our lives to understand and emulate.

With that, always, always remember that there is more. There is more in Christ than we know. There is more in your relationships than what you currently see. There is more in your potential than you are currently experiencing. Jesus intended greatness for us, and if things aren't great right now, it's not over yet. I encourage you to run after Christ with all you have, to never give up on searching for your true identity until you've figured it out. Connect with the heart of God and ask Him what He thinks of you, what He wants for you. Work through your relationships, love people, be intentional, and learn to love yourself. All of this takes time, and I haven't figured it all out, yet I know that what is coming for you is so much greater than what currently is.

**What is one thing God spoke to you while reading this chapter, and what steps are you going to take to engage Him more in this area?**

_____

_____

_____

_____

_____

## ACKNOWLEDGEMENTS

Writing a book is one thing but getting a book published is another. So, I first have to thank United House Publishing and their entire team for partnering with my dream and helping to get it out to the world. Guys, you wouldn't have wanted to read the first version of this book, so thank them that it's legible and you can enjoy it now. Thank you, Amber, for being a friend and answering my crazy 3 a.m. texts. Thank you, Natasha, for being a partner and a coach throughout this book journey. Thank you, Charity, Caitlyn, Kristin, Erin, and all of the other members of the UHP team that had a hand in this project – each of you sowed something into this book that will change lives.

**Jeffrey Trudeau:** You are the most supportive husband in the world; I am confident of that. From the moment you walked me through discovering my identity in Him, to the moments that you sat next to me as I attempted to share this message with the world, you never once gave up on me – even when I wanted to give up on myself. Thank you for feeding me Slim Jim's late into the night as I wrote and for always being willing to celebrate the small "wins" along the way. I love you more than you could know, and I can't wait to change the world together.

**Drew and Melissa Neal**: You are both ridiculously encouraging. You believe in people when they don't believe in themselves, and I can truly say you've impacted my life in the best way, so, thank you. Thank you for believing in me, my vision, my dreams, and my desires. Thank you for teaching me the character of a loving God and for demonstrating Jesus in every facet of your lives. This dream wouldn't have happened without you.

**Mom**: Thank you for always encouraging me to go after the dreams in my heart—even if that dream was to be a singer on American Idol and my lack of experience told you I would only make it to Hollywood as a janitor. Thank you for never failing to tell me how important I was to you—important enough for you to miss a trip to Paris to adopt me (If I make a bunch from these books, I'll take you).

**Daddy**: I can't even express how thankful I am for our special relationship. Thank you for giving up so much to show me how important I am to you. I've never doubted your love for me, and it's that support that has gotten me to where I am today. Thank you for fixing every old and broken car I ever drove (and consequently crashed), I'd like to take the credit for your amazing mechanic skills, since you had to use them so much between the years of 2011-2014. You're welcome.

**Rachel Bell**: Thank you for answering all my late-night texts, for sitting with me when I wasn't feeling my best, and for encouraging me forward into what God has for me. Each Target trip we took changed my life for the better—including the one where you told me you were pregnant.

**Shelby Palazzolo**: Thank you for listening to me vent and for trusting me with what's going on in your life. I love you like a sister. I'm glad you got over hating me when I was the annoying younger cousin so that now we can be friends... you are over that, right?

**Kelli Youngert**: You're the best, best-friend/sister-in-law I ever could have asked for. Thank you for just being there when I needed someone to grab a Starbucks and walk with me in circles around Target. I feel like all that walking sufficiently replaced the gym trips we were supposed to do.

**Travis Gergen**: Thank you for being THE BEST encourager and for dealing with my hangry sass. Also, thanks for reading this now and thinking how much you miss Michigan and how you should come back and visit.

There are many more that I could list, but I am running out of space. This entire process has taken a team, and I truly have no idea how I could have done this without these people. I am forever grateful for each of you, and the many more that encouraged me along the way. I feel so empowered knowing I have so many supportive people around me.

Thank you all from the bottom of my heart.

# NOTES

1)   Ford, Henry. "Whether You Believe You Can Do a Thing or Not, You Are Right." Quote Investigator, Accessed November 30, 2018. https://quoteinvestigator.com/2015/02/03/you-can/

## ABOUT THE AUTHOR

Miranda Trudeau is an author and a speaker who has a passion to encourage young adults in their identity as they make powerful decisions in their lives. After growing up in the church, Miranda went on to become involved in leadership for both children's and youth ministry at a local church, where these moments defined her passion to see everyone, especially young adults, discover their true identity in Christ.

www.ingramcontent.com/pod-product-compliance
Lightning Source LLC
LaVergne TN
LVHW052028080426
835513LV00018B/2214